Veterans In Paradise

The Veterans Guide To Moving Abroad

3rd Edition

John H Davis

Contents

Foreword

Four out of ten Americans at some point consider moving abroad and well over ten million Americans live abroad. I'm leading with that to let you know that you aren't crazy for reading this book and considering moving overseas. If you're a fellow Veteran, then a better life at half the cost is possible. For some of us, we can live healthier, happier and more peaceful lives abroad. Moving overseas is more doable than ever before, and this book is designed to provide a pathway to a better life for my fellow Veterans because we deserve it.

The American dream was designed for us and yet less and less Veterans are living that dream. The phrase was coined by historian James Adams in his book *The Epic of America* where he defined it as, *"that dream of a land in which life should be better and richer and fuller for everyone, with opportunity for each according to ability or achievement."* The concept comes from our own Declaration of Independence which states that we have the right to life, liberty and the pursuit of happiness. I moved abroad because I want that American dream, but outside America because the American Dream ain't quite what it used to be.

The rising cost of quality living in the country we fought for is making life harder for Veterans. Financial stress is a major problem in America and contributes to the worsening mental health crisis. The percentage of

Americans that call themselves *"very happy"* has been steadily declining since the 1950's. A lot of Veterans think the way they're currently living is the only way and I'm here to tell you that it's not. Your adventure isn't over yet.

Living abroad after retiring from the Army has greatly benefited my mental, emotional, financial, and spiritual health. Like a lot of Veterans, maybe like you, I didn't have an easy time transitioning out of the military. I had meltdowns, got divorced, called the suicide hotline drunk, overused medications and spent a night in jail.

I had been so consumed by my military identity; I had no clue who I was without the uniform. Taking off those dog tags was like ripping away a piece of my soul. I felt lost and feeling lost is a terrible fucking feeling, especially when you feel lost in your own hometown. I was suffocating.

I ended up in *Veteran Purgatory*, this is where you're not in the military but not comfortable in civilian life. It's an unhealthy mental space where you feel out of place and lost in your own life. I felt like I was living someone else's life. I became an adult in the military, it was all I knew. My PTSD symptoms never really hit me until I got out of the military and they hit me hard.

I went to the Dominican Republic on a vacation and realized that for the first time in a long time, I was sleeping through the night, less anxious and I felt something I hadn't felt since I was a kid. I felt peace, it felt fucking good. I realized living abroad could be my new lifestyle, I could have freedom, pursue my writing and work on my PTSD.

I canceled my return ticket and decided to extend my vacation a bit. Then I started meeting other Veterans, who like me, got addicted to that peaceful Caribbean vibe. I was shocked to discover there were already thousands of American Veterans living in the Dominican Republic. A fellow Veteran helped me find a nice little one-bedroom apartment for $475 a month and at the time I was paying $2,700 in Boston. I started living my life outdoors in the sun, picked up scuba diving and was eating fresh food. I spent more time in nature and started slowing down and enjoying the little things in life. I started learning Spanish and before long I was hooked on life in paradise.

The Veterans abroad world opened up to me. I found out that we had medical centers in the Dominican Republic that treat American Veterans. I discovered that the American Legion and Veterans of Foreign Wars have posts all over the world. I learned that we can still get our VA compensation abroad, we can get healthcare abroad and even use our GI Bill.

I decided to stay in the Dominican Republic. I had to do a quick trip back to the states to throw away, sell or donate everything I owned. I sold my truck, my motorcycle, my furniture and all the possessions I gathered over the years.

I put a box of military keepsakes in my mom's basement and that was that. I had nothing but a suitcase with some T-shirts, my passport and my computer. I did have something that I hadn't had in a while, a shit ton of hope, optimism and excitement at this coming chapter in my life.

I started sharing some of my life on social media after a few months and I was surprised, although I probably shouldn't have been, that a lot of Veterans were interested. People I deployed with were calling me like:

"Dude, how do I do it?"

"Will I lose my VA Benefits?"

"How do I get healthcare?"

"What about my kids and schools?"

"Is it dangerous?"

"How do visas work?"

I started helping Veterans move abroad, it became my new mission. I set out to let Veterans know that we could live healthier and happier abroad. It was something no other Veteran was doing, and it was fun. The first Veteran that I helped saw me post some photos on my Facebook and he came down, I gave him a tour of the town, took him to the Veteran centers and helped him get an apartment.

It changed his life and in thirty days he transformed into an entirely new person. His PTSD diminished, he was happy, and he was getting healthy. He went from surviving to thriving and in a short period of time he was absolutely unrecognizable.

Veterans were curious about moving abroad. I wrote the first edition of this book, the one you're reading now and turned it into a quick PDF on my website. After I wrote it, I wanted to update and improve the information when I realized how many Veterans needed this information.

I went to Costa Rica, met with the American Legion there and the Marine Corp League and wrote about why Costa Rica was an awesome place for Veterans. I interviewed Veterans living in Thailand and met with the VFW there. I traveled around, from the Philippines to Africa and was I discovered there was an enormous number of Veterans living their best lives outside of the country we fought for.

I set out to be the bridge to connect Veterans in the states to the life they deserve in paradise. Moving abroad as a Veteran isn't just about continually vacationing, it's about achieving balance, peace and living a fulfilling life. It's about the life that you deserve, without the bullshit.

We're Just Getting Started

When I got out of the military, I was worried my glory days were behind me. A lot of us look back at our military days with a certain nostalgia. If you're a fan of *The Office* like me, think back to Andy saying, *"I wish there was a way to know you're in the good ol' days before you actually left them."*

Moving abroad put me in the mentality where I wasn't looking backward, I wasn't anxious about the future but instead I was enjoying the moment and living life to the fullest. I was doing things I never thought I'd do, like enjoying a sunset and appreciating the little the little things. To really maximize your life, timing matters.

To have great experiences, you generally need three things: *Time, Money, and Health*. But health naturally declines with age, you aren't going to be as healthy at seventy as you are at fifty. The American system is designed for you to work yourself into the nursing home. Then when you hit that point, you might have the time and money to do the things you've always wanted to do. Moving abroad changes the math and you're able to live the life that you deserve after your military service.

Myself and Keith Pyron, AKA SGT Sosua[1] created our Veterans in Paradise[2] organization in the Dominican Republic and started hosting events. We're putting out free information, a newsletter and connecting Veterans

---

[1] Subscribe to SGT Sosua on YouTube at: https://www.youtube.com/@SGTSosua

[2] Veteransinparadise.com is our website where you can sign up for the free newsletter and more.

with the kind of lives they deserve. The vision is a collaborative group of Veterans living in the Dominican Republic to support one another abroad. We do more than just have beers together on the beach, we help Vets with everything they need to know moving abroad so they can be part of a thriving military community abroad. Our secondary mission is to give back to the communities here, especially the youth on the North Coast of the Dominican Republic.

This book is going to be an idea generator for you, to inspire you, to get you from the life you have to the life you want. We're expected to live our lives a certain way, to work away the best years of our lives, to buy shit we don't need to impress people we don't like.

American society has transformed from citizens into consumers, consuming materialism, toxic news, stupid social media content and politics. But Veterans are the type of people who walk the path less traveled, we're willing to throw ourselves into the unknown, we're adaptable and strategic. We are the 1%.

I'm writing this book primarily to Veterans and our families, but much of the information here is useful to anyone. If you're a police officer, federal agent, border patrol, firefighter or anyone in those types of first responder fields - you'll find a lot of truth in these pages. My own opinions are going to be here and probably more than a few curse words.

I'm not seeking political correctness or writing to sensitive people. I'm writing to Veterans to make a difference. I don't see our government or military leadership doing enough to confront the reality that our toughest battles weren't in the streets of Iraq or the mountains of Afghanistan, they were instead coming home.

Veterans are people and we all kind of want the same things. We want to be happy. Moving abroad made me happy, I want to share with you why it could be what you're looking for too.

Disclaimer

The world is constantly changing and in an instant things can shift. There are natural disasters, pandemics, wars, elections and world events. Everything regarding international travel conditions, laws, visas to cost of living information is subject to change. This book is a collection of personal experiences, research, and interviews designed to explore and inform Veterans moving and considering moving abroad.

Currencies can rise and fall, places that were safe can become dangerous and if there's any constant in the human experience, it's change. Ensure you get secondary verification of any specific information before making major decisions. I'm not an immigration attorney, doctor, or financial adviser. What I am is a Veteran who found a higher quality of life moving abroad and I wanted to share that with my brothers and sisters in arms. This book is for informational purposes only.

When I created the first edition of this, I made it free because I felt the information was necessary. The second edition was free, and the third edition you're reading is going to keep that tradition. I live in the real world like anyone, I still need beer and rent money, but my mission is to help Veterans. I don't want to safeguard this information.

Although slightly cliche, I want to sincerely thank you for your service because I've been there, through the bullshit and pain of it all. This book is available in two formats, the free PDF and a hardcover on Amazon. I still prefer a book in my hands, opposed to reading on a screen. If you did buy the physical copy, I appreciate your support.

No endorsement is intended of one product, service, group, service or whatever else by their inclusion or exclusion. This book has a lot of links to provide additional information to assist you in your decision-making process. But links to bad, get adjusted and things change. There are zero advertisements here and no promotional bullshit, if I'm shouting something out it's because I want to and I think it provides value. If you've got further resources to include, I'll include them in future editions or on my blog or newsletter.

I'm not encouraging you or telling you to move abroad. I'm telling you my story and providing information, guidance, and suggestions based on years of living abroad. Moving abroad isn't for most people, but the military isn't for most people either.

On my social media, website and blog I have further information about moving and living abroad as an American Veteran. Check me out on social media. I'd appreciate any sharing, following, liking and all that jazz.

Chapter 1

The Veteran Expat

America has always made enormous demands of its warrior class. From our grandfathers who fought in WW2, to my uncle in Vietnam to myself in Afghanistan, not much has changed. The War on Terror generation of Veterans is undergoing a collective identity crisis in the aftermath of our conflicts, kind of a *"What the fuck?"* moment. There was no finding WMD's in Iraq, no matter how hard we looked. There was no winning the war in Afghanistan, especially the way we were fighting it.

The struggles within our Veteran community aren't a secret. Veteran suicide has become as American as apple pie and it doesn't seem like the people running things care much about it. We fought in our nation's longest wars and then reemerged into a society that feels like it's at war with itself. Many of us feel out of place, unhappy and struggle in the country that we fought for.

We are communal people, Veterans prioritize teamwork. During our basic training and boot camp the military takes young men and women from all over, different backgrounds, races, and classes and forges them into brothers and sisters that would die for one another. That's not replicated in any other aspect of our society.

Veterans are the most diverse group in the country, spanning every race, religion, hometown and background. We range from seventeen to over a hundred years old. Political division doesn't separate us during our service; we live in solidarity in pursuit of a higher mission. Then we get out of the military and find ourselves in an American society more fucked up than we are.

The concept of moving abroad as a Veteran might seem confusing to some. People on social media, Veterans included, will comment things like *"You're supposed to stay and fight for the country"* and *"You abandoned America."* I'm not really sure what I'm supposed to do, I thought those years in Afghanistan I was fighting for the country. At least I thought so at the time, now I'm not so sure.

The term Veteran expat might make some people shake their heads, because we're Americans! We're the country people move to, not the country people move from.

The more you think about it, the more you realize Veterans make the perfect expats. We're already used to traveling and we're used to different cultures. We are used to moving and living abroad during our military years. There are military bases in around 80 countries and troops are often stationed in Germany, Japan, South Korea, Italy, the Middle East and all over the world. Sometimes during those stationed abroad experiences, we fall in love with where we're living and that's why there's always a high concentration of Veteran expats around military bases abroad.

We're used to blending into different cultures, we fit ourselves into military culture which is a world of its own. It has its own language, acronyms, uniforms and way of life. It's not wrong to say our proud military culture is as foreign to some Americans as Mongolian culture. We live in a different reality, on almost another plane of existence during our military service.

We had to learn how to be adaptable, because military culture has its own set of norms and expectations, as does Japanese culture, Muslim culture and Brazilian culture. We learned how to thrive and succeed in the most difficult of environments with minimal support. That's why when I downgraded into a small apartment in the Dominican Republic, within walking distance of the beach, restaurants, bars and a gym, I was happier than I've ever been in my adult life.

There used to be a Veteran in every family, now there isn't and that hasn't been good for our country. The military is a culture of respect and Veterans know how to respect people, places and things. Even if we don't understand or agree, we're capable of showing respect. We've all shown respect to people in the military, standing at attention or parade rest to people whom we secretly despised.

When I was a squad leader after my second deployment, my platoon had a lieutenant that could get lost on the way to Starbucks but through it all, I respected him for his position, saluted him and called him Sir. This guy couldn't find a map with a map, but he was still in charge. A Veteran expat is going to respect the country they choose, the laws and cultural norms. You're going to bow to people all the time in Thailand, dress appropriately in the Middle East, remove your shoes before entering a house in Japan, learn a few local phrases where you're at and be helpful to the elderly everywhere.

We're trained to leave things better than we found them, I'm proud to say Veterans volunteer more than anyone. My Veteran organization in the Dominican Republic, Veterans in Paradise donates to local public schools. The VFW in Thailand supports local orphanages and Veterans are doing everything around the world from environmental cleanups of the Indian Ocean to rescuing animals in Costa Rica.

Veteran expats give back, we're grateful people and if you're moving abroad there's a lot of ways to give back. One of the cool things about making a difference abroad is that you can have a big impact for a little bit of money. In the United States, it's just gotten to the point where it feels like if you give a homeless person a crisp twenty-dollar bill, they look at you like, *"What am I supposed to do with this?"* Overseas that twenty dollars can go a long way.

Expat Or Immigrant?

An Expatriate is a person residing outside of their home country, expat for short. The Veteran expat is a military Veteran who chooses to live outside of the country they fought for. I want to make definitions somewhat clear because I don't consider myself an immigrant, I consider myself an expat and there's a difference. One can be both an expat and an immigrant at different points in their lives.

I have a friend who was born in Mexico, immigrated to the United States, served in the military for twenty years and retired back to Mexico as an expat. I consider myself an expat because I still retain American citizenship, wherever I'm at I'm probably not there forever and immigrant has a more permanent feel to it. The people who immigrate to America in pursuit of a better life are immigrants, they intend to stay in the United States and build a life there.

A general rule of thumb is that if you move to a country in which you have an economic advantage, you're an expat. Globally, hundreds of millions of people live outside their country of birth from migrant workers to refugees. Their experiences differ greatly from mine and are more about survival and economic opportunities. I'm not writing about that.

I'm writing because I want the American dream, but outside America. I'm explaining how I define the phrase

Veteran Expat because you'll see that word throughout the book and not the word immigrant. People will say on social media *"you're an immigrant, not an expat"* as I talk about my life abroad. The key difference is in the intention behind moving countries, I'm moving for a better life utilizing military benefits, personal resources and online income.

Veterans deserve better than what we've received, both from our citizens and government. The reality is that with your military benefits, you can live a high-quality life outside the United States. There are many classes of Veteran Expats.

There's the military retiree who realized he can live a millionaire style life abroad with their retirement and benefits. Then the younger Veteran Expat who works online as a digital nomad after an enlistment or two. Then you've got Veteran families who might be fed up with public schooling in the United States and want to raise their kids elsewhere. You've got the Veteran Expat who met a local while stationed in South Korea and decided to get married and live there opposed to the United States. You've got Veterans that work for the United Nations, or other international organizations or do military contracting abroad. You've got the divorced Veteran Expat who takes their 100% VA Compensation and lives on a beach in the Philippines.

Just as in the military, there's no stereotype. I've met every kind of Veteran abroad, from single females to families of seven to a Vietnam Vet in Thailand with a wife half his age. Being a Veteran expat is living your life on your terms; it's having you cake and eating it too. It's embracing life, it's throwing out norms and taking the bull by the horns. It's scary at times, just like the military is because you're out in the world without a safety net. You're pursuing the life that you want, on a mission of your own creation. Even without the military pushing you, you're stepping outside your comfort zone by moving abroad, it's a rush.

You're opening yourself up to the unknown and living in the now. Getting out of the military made me feel like I was always somehow mentally trapped in the past or the future, I couldn't retain focus on the present. There was always some future problem to solve, a to-do list that kept growing or I was battling my PTSD.

Knowing if you're ready to move abroad in some ways is like knowing if you're ready to join the military. But the key difference is that if you don't like it abroad, you can go home. You can't just up and quit the military by buying a plane ticket back home. I've come across a lot of Veterans who say they wish they had moved abroad or did a year of travel when they got out of the military or that they wish they had the courage. Don't live your life with regrets.

Everyone's circumstances are different, I'm a no wife, no kids, no pets, no plants, no debt, no problems type of Veteran. Obviously, it's easier for me than most to move abroad. There are going to be challenges if you want to do this and bumps in the road. People are going to call you crazy, your family probably won't understand and at times you'll even question yourself.

I love America and the advantages, benefits and opportunities I've received by privilege of my birth. I've spent years of my life in the military and in Afghanistan, I've worked in education in Africa, I've taught English in Thailand and traveled throughout the world, and I know I hit the lottery being born in the good ol' US of A. Then I won a second lottery and got a golden ticket leaving America because I have the benefits without the drawbacks.

Moving abroad as a Veteran is about as much of a fresh start as you'll ever get. If you're a Veteran, I know you've fucked up a bit here and there. We've made mistakes, wasted money, ruined relationships and done things in the past we're embarrassed about now. Moving abroad is forgiving yourself and leaving the past in the past, you can leave your problems at customs and board that plane. You can put your best foot forward without the weight of the past, there's real beauty in moving abroad as a Veteran and starting anew in a foreign land. You're a modern-day Viking, a crusader, an explorer and you're conquering.

The Veteran expat life goes deeper than just a desire for cheaper shit and going out to dinner for a reasonable cost. Veterans want less combative lives after our service, we want peace, we want nature, we want to be able to heal. For a small percentage of Veterans who have that adventurous spirit, we can live higher quality lives outside of the United States. Maybe even lives are a hell of a lot more fun. Welcome to the Veteran expat life.

Chapter 2

Pushin' and Pullin'

Leaving your previous life behind and starting anew somewhere else has always been a normal part of humanity, we've always migrated. Mankind has traveled for war and peace, to escape religious persecution, for freedom, politics and resources. With the exception of forced migration through slavery, we've left our homes for a pretty simple reason: The hope of a better life elsewhere. Humanity started hitting the road with Homo Erectus traveling out of Africa 1.75 million years ago and Homo Sapiens (us) only made it to what we call *"The America's"* fifteen to twenty thousand years ago.

There are two different factors when it comes to leaving your homeland, push and pull. Push factors are what drives you to new lands, that's traditionally been things like war, famine, drought, persecution and the like. Push factors are associated with the country of origin and are what convinces you maybe the grass is greener on the other side. Pull factors are related to the destination, what's attracting you to this place over others or staying put. A lot might come to mind but it's important to understand your *"Why"* when it comes to moving abroad both in why you want to go and why you want to go to a specific place.

Push

Modern American push factors would include high cost of living, mass shootings, political division, public education and whatever else might be your motivation to leave. For some Democrats, Donald Trump might be a push factors, for Republicans it's Democrats. A push factor for you might be the toxic dating culture in the United States or the cancerous chemicals in our food. My Veteran friend who left California was sick of the wildfires and homeless people, so those pushed him away. My Veteran friend in upstate New York was sick of the cold and property taxes, so those drove him out. Your push factors are going to be somewhat unique to you, but most of them involve money and whatever else it is that you're tired of. From school shootings to escaping the rat race to the high cost of living.

Pull

Pull factors are what's pulling you towards a new country, like a fish on a line. Traditionally these have been religious freedom, resources, safety, economic and land opportunities and a better life for children. Modern pull factors for Veteran Expats aren't necessarily within historical norms but are important to understand. These pull factors might include better weather, lower cost of living, more homogeneous society, fresher food, less stress, cultural experiences, adventure, a fresh start and whatever pulls you towards your dream location.

My pull factors in the Dominican Republic were scuba diving, beaches, walkability and a Veteran community. Your pull factors towards Japan might be sushi, cleanliness and respect. Your pull factors towards Brazil might be Jiu Jitsu, cheap living and a better dating culture. For my Veteran friend in Argentina, he loves mountain climbing and red wine, so those things pulled him in. Your pull factors are important in determining where you want to move.

Every Veteran Expat has something of a superhero expat origin story about why they left the states. The overall theme, at least in my experience is *"I was sick of the bullshit."* My story was when I was in graduate school in Boston and they shut down the bars and gyms, then I was told I would be completing the rest of my degree online. I grew up in Iowa, I was only in Boston for school and had no reason to stay there. I was going to get Boston BAH for the rest of my degree program, so I started looking at getting the hell out of Boston.

Going back home to Iowa was unappealing and the country was in the midst of losing its mind during the pandemic. The Dominican Republic was one of the few countries accepting tourists and it was in the same time zone as Boston so I could do my Zoom classes at normal times. Getting that Boston BAH and living in the

Dominican Republic during the pandemic was a pretty good deal and I fell in love with the country, people, music and beaches. A ten-day trip turned into a three month stay and that was almost four years ago now.

Aaron in the Philippines

I love the people here. Everyone is very kind and everyone in my neighborhood helps each other out. I live on a smaller island here and I can go island hopping pretty much whenever I want. My rent is $300 a month so you can't really beat that. Last week I don't think I put on a shirt one time, and I just live this beach bum life. I get to go fishing every day. I don't know if I'll stay forever but I've been here three years now and I can't see myself going back to America. Everyone here also speaks English so that's been an easier transition then when I was stationed in Japan. There are lots of Veterans here, most of them are older than me but I have a few Veteran friends to hang out with.

Catherine in Costa Rica

I teach yoga here in Costa Rica, the entire country is amazing. If you're a female Vet I think this is one of the best places to be. The Pura Vida life hits you and you never want to leave. The country also doesn't have a military, it's one of the few in the world so that's kind of interesting to be totally separate from that type of culture. There is amazing nature here and I've found more healing in nature than anything the VA ever gave me. There's an American Legion in San Jose, but that's kind of far from me and I don't really interact with them. It's good to know though for other Veterans. I picked up Spanish and I have a Costa Rican boyfriend here, we surf and do yoga and it's a good life.

Sylvester in the Dominican Republic

I moved here when I heard about the Veteran healthcare clinics. I live in Puerto Plata and go to one here, it's really been a lifechanging experience for my back and my feet. I got healthy, sober and I'm living my best life. I'm surrounded by beautiful people and I feel peace here living next to the ocean. I want to ask Veterans, what are you waiting for?

Jumping In The Deep End

Moving abroad can be a terrifying proposition, even when you know in your heart it's what you want, it can be tough to pull that trigger. You're going to be looked at as certifiably insane by some people when you make the move. Prepare yourself for lots of hate, doubt and a bunch of jealousy. You'll hear a lot, *"Oh I wish I could do something like that."* There's going to be people who try to talk you out of it, it'll probably feel a lot like when you joined the military.

My mother was not thrilled when I let her know I had dropped out of college and was joining the Army. Fifteen years later she also informed me she didn't think it was smart to rent an apartment in the Dominican Republic or even leave the resort. Sometimes you shouldn't listen to mom or anyone else.

We all have a fear of the unknown but if you're reading this then you're already not like most people. When you raised your right hand and swore to uphold and defend the constitution, you signed up to put your life on the line. You accepted the fact that you might die for your beliefs, your country and your brothers and sisters in arms. Moving abroad is throwing yourself back into the unknown but we're fortunate to have more information than ever. Maybe even too much information and it's hard to know what to believe and what not to, especially on social media platforms which is one reason why I wanted to write this. I don't want to sell some unrealistic dream, I want to give you a no bullshit perspective that includes the challenges.

There's no magic button to push to get a window into your future in ten years, to see if this moved worked or didn't work for you. Some Veterans move abroad only to move back, sometimes it's just time to move home or things don't work out. There's nothing wrong with that, I'm abroad now but I don't know what the future holds. The truth is that if you're thinking about moving abroad, you're halfway to execution because the majority of people would never even entertain it. Just like the majority of people would never join the military.

Whatever is pushing you and pulling you is going to be unique to you. Moving abroad is going to wipe the slate clean and allow you to write the next chapter of your life. You can be whoever the hell you want in a lot of ways, you can redefine yourself and your priorities. You can be your best self and take forward what you want and leave behind what you don't.

The military is the most effective preparation for expat life. Much of your training, habits, discipline and values will help you thrive abroad. There's no tried-and-true recipe for moving abroad, no perfect plan or program to follow. I'll lay out a lot of information, but everyone's life is different. We're all coming from and going to different places, there's going to be lots of ideas that will benefit you, save you money and help you make the best decision for yourself and your future.

Chapter 3

Your Fresh Start

There's real beauty in a fresh start and sometimes as a Veteran you need one. An opportunity to start over without the weight of the past, people's perceptions of you or your history. Being a Veteran expat is the ultimate reset button, there's fresh hope, optimism and infinite possibilities. You are truly the architect of your life when you set foot in your new country.

One reason I've always thought Veterans struggle is because we live too much in the past. But none of the past needs to happen ever again if we don't want it to. Going overseas lets you see the world with new eyes, there's a real sense of wonder to it all. A fresh start isn't limited to New Years Day, it can be whenever you want. Every day abroad to me feels like a new fresh start and an opportunity for anything and everything.

Moving abroad lets you leave old habits behind and pick up new ones but there's no such thing as truly starting from scratch. Even if you lose every dime you have, you still have your military and life experiences. You still have your lessons and values. You're a phoenix moving abroad, rising from the ashes of your old life to start a new one.

You're going to be in a new place where anything is possible, it's a chance to be who you want to be.

In the military we're trained to put everything before ourselves. The mission comes first; your battle buddies come first, the country comes first. Your needs and wants are barely an afterthought. We get used to that and often take that mentality into our lives post service. We sacrifice for everything and everyone, we're willing to do it because that's what warriors do. But there comes a time and point where you realize it's time to serve yourself. The military will take and take. Your friends and family will take and take if you let them, the rat race will steal your life away and it goes on and on. When you put other people first, they get used to you coming second. Moving abroad is making yourself a priority, it's serving yourself.

My friend James recently moved to the Dominican Republic, he had just turned sixty and determined he had about one or two decent decades left before the grave. He confided in me that he lived every day of his life for other people, he lived for twenty years for the Marine Corps. He lived for his ex-wife and kids. He lived for his mother, supporting her until she passed, and he lived for his family. James never thought much about what he wanted, he was always serving others. Then on his sixtieth birthday he realized he was alone, his kids had grown up, he was divorced and his service to his beloved Marine Corp was over.

James sat there on his birthday and nobody called him, there was no cake and he reflected where to go from there. He reached out to me via social media, and we talked about him moving abroad. A week later he was in the Dominican Republic and found himself a nice apartment and created a new life for himself. He says he's living the last third of his life for him and I'm here for it.

The dangers of taking too much risk are obvious but we don't hear many warnings about playing it too safe. To a lot of people, moving abroad seems like a crazy and brave thing to do. But staying put, doing the same thing day in and out, being trapped in an office, being bored or being plugged into the matrix felt like a far riskier venture. I always knew I could come back if things didn't work out abroad. I had my American passport as a safety net.

Playing it safe is limiting, you can't make a game winning shot if you never take one. There's value in the attempt, in the game winning shot or moving abroad or starting a business. Rejection and failure are normal parts of life, this last week I had a book rejected by a publisher and was rejected by a pretty girl. Both are learning experiences and even though rejection stings, I can come back and try again. People rarely regret moving abroad just like they rarely regret joining the military.

Getting a fresh start in the same environment is difficult. For things to change, things have to change. Often what we want out of a change in scenery is a change in ourselves. Moving to a new country isn't going to be an instant reinvention, you can't run away from yourself, but it presents an opportunity for personal evolution.

We never make all the right decisions or get as lucky as we want but some of us are a lot closer to our potential than others. A lot of who we are is influenced by where we are. I've put a lot of thought into how your environment impacts mental health and PTSD and the reality is if you want to grow and heal, it's harder in a toxic environment. If a plant isn't getting the right nutrients, it won't grow. If you put a fish in a small tank, it can only grow to the size of the aquarium. Maybe some of your problems aren't you, maybe it's your environment.

A lot of the people that surround us aren't happy. We feed off people's emotions and if everywhere you look people are stressed and depressed, it's going to rub off on you. Two years ago, Gallup rated America as the 15th happiest country in the world. Last year we came in at 23rd and with the political craziness and rising cost of living I bet we will continue to slide down the list. Happiness is a relative concept and a lot of factors play into it, but it doesn't feel like we're a nation at peace.

To Veterans, the idea of a life without a little adrenaline and excitement is boring. A lot of people grow up, work, get married, retire and die in the same city. Almost a quarter of Americans will never own a passport or travel internationally. There's the American dream but then there's also the Veteran dream; to live the best life you can post service. That's what moving abroad is, an opportunity for you to live the Veteran expat dream.

Chapter 4

Should You Stay Or Go?

Moving abroad is a deeply personal decision. It's normal to fluctuate a little bit in your decision-making process and go back and forth. There are days you'll be itching to get the hell out on a one-way ticket and days you want to stay in America forever. There are some questions to ask yourself and the only answer can come from the person in the mirror. There are personal questions like *"Will I be able to make friends?"* and more logistical, *"How do I manage my money abroad?"*

If you're considering moving abroad though, you must address the negatives. That's why sometimes expat message boards are better places for information than bullshit social media videos. You'll meet plenty of expats in these groups who complain, are depressed, and it's not working out for them. Some of these people should have never moved abroad in the first place. Kind of like how some people shouldn't ever have joined the military, nothing is for everyone.

A lot of expats head abroad only to head back, but most don't regret trying the experience. Moving abroad is a big step outside your comfort zone, and it can be difficult to adapt. Languages are hard to learn, cultures difficult to understand, and being an expat has moments of extreme frustration. Moving abroad is inconvenient; there's no getting around that. It's like Michael Scott in *The Office* when he's scared to move because he won't know the new TV channels in Colorado. You won't have proximity to your relatives, you'll miss your friends, and your favorite restaurants aren't going to move with you.

A lot of the online influencer crowd makes living abroad seem like a magical escape to a fantasy land of luxury. There are carefully selected photos and edited video reels showing how you can live better for cheaper in a foreign land. You've probably seen the *Instagram vs Reality* content. Real life isn't ever perfect, you aren't going to be sipping wine with ocean views every second of your life abroad. Unfortunately, you'll still have bills to pay, taxes to file and laundry to do.

The People I See Get In The Most Trouble Usually...

- Didn't do an adequate trial run.
- They spend too much time comparing.
- They can't separate from American perceptions of time.
- They embrace a party/vacation lifestyle and succumb to vices.
- They're moving abroad just for the saving money aspect, not to enjoy the culture.

- They're not comfortable being alone.
- They expect to build community and feel at home immediately.
- Family issues in the states drive them home.
- Frustration with bureaucracy, language difficulties, and culture shock.
- They have a few bad days and it sours the whole experience.

Expat life requires a lot out of you, but the most important quality is adaptability. The environment isn't going to shift to meet you, you have to transform yourself. You can't expect your new city and country to be where you came from. Your there because it's different.

Going overseas is embracing the adventure and saying yes to the wild side of life, if you're too stuck in your ways then moving abroad isn't for you. During the planning stage of moving abroad, a lot of people overthink it. You'll never be 100% perfectly prepared and there will always be unknowns. Even living abroad for years, I still run into problems because that's what life is.

There are going to be downsides to moving abroad, you aren't going to have the same rights you have in America. There aren't going to be Veteran discounts at stores, you'll miss your favorite restaurant and even Netflix will have different content. A lot of Veteran Expats struggle with loneliness, time differences and making friends. There are signs you should move abroad and some signs to keep your ass where you're at. I talk to a lot of Veterans about moving abroad and often have to pump the brakes on some unrealistic dreams.

The average person takes one to two vacations a year, that's about 15 days out of 365. If you're the type of person who hates flying home after a vacation and contemplates canceling the return ticket, then you might be ready to give living abroad a try. A lot of Veterans love the idea of living abroad, but reality differs from expectations. You are leaving everything you know behind and experiencing lots of change.

You're going to struggle to adjust, you might not know the language, culture or food. There are alternatives besides just moving abroad, gap years aren't only for rich kids or college students. Taking a few months to slow travel SE Asia or backpacking Europe can be a good reset. You can also live abroad for part of the year, like in the winter and live in the states the rest of the time. I've always viewed travel as an underrated therapy for the Veteran community.

People think of travel as fun, it's drinking pina coladas on a beach. When you're in the military, you're constantly on the move, told where to go and even for how long. They even give you a list of what to pack. If you've ever served, you know the military has the unique ability to remove the joy from everything.

You might be traveling, but you're sleeping on uncomfortable cots, jammed into buses, planes, trucks, and even cattle cars. You're hurrying up then waiting, you're told to be somewhere at 0400 to wait around until 1600. Plus, someone is always yelling, and your pilot never tells you to sit back and enjoy the flight because they know you're not going to.

Even the simple act of planning a future trip reduces stress and makes you feel better. Traveling is one way for veterans to disconnect from our stress and reconnect with ourselves. We never feel fully settled in military life, that call to pick up and go can come at any time. Maybe you're thinking you've had enough traveling during your military career, but Veterans should be better at enjoying the freedom we've fought for. We fight for freedom but sometimes feel like the least free Americans.

Through travel, veterans can reflect on where we've been and most importantly, where we want to go. Because the military isn't the end of our adventures, it was just the beginning and now the destination is up to you. You've got amazing stories from the military; you've gone places and done things the average person will never do. Traveling keeps your legend going.

Traveling is one of the most underrated stress relievers and veterans during vacations report diminished PTSD symptoms. They sleep better, struggle less with anxiety, and can relax. There's no such thing as a permanent vacation, but travel therapy is real therapy. If you're feeling burnt out, even the smallest of getaways can provide a much-needed reset.

Veterans value experiences more than things. If we were materialistic, we wouldn't have joined the military to begin with. I first started solo traveling in Thailand, my hostel was nine bucks a night and most meals rang in under three dollars. It was scary as hell the first time going somewhere alone, I was trained to always have backup. But then I realized I could do whatever the hell I wanted, all the time, when I was by myself. You and I never got to control our destinations in the military, we went wherever Uncle Sam sent us. Traveling lets Veterans reclaim our freedom.

A lot of people go right to the edge and almost join the military but veterans are far from almost people. We don't belong on the couch, we belong where the action is. The adventures in your life aren't over when you get out of the military. If you don't have a passport, it's time to apply.

Is It Worth It?

Should you stay or should you go? I'll be the first to tell you that moving abroad can be a confusing and overwhelming process. You'll probably go back and forth a hundred times and some days you'll want to get the hell out and some days stay in America forever. Living abroad requires you being a home for yourself in a lot of ways, no matter where you're at physically. We tend to live in a world where the grass is greener on the other side, and we always want to be where we're not.

We make the world a lot smaller than it needs to be. Living abroad is a paradigm shifting, perspective altering experience that feels like you're viewing the world for the first time. Leaving America is escaping the matrix and reinventing your life on your terms. Being an expat is taking your life firmly in your own hands, being captain of your own ship, and master of your fate.

As an expat, you're able to live in two different worlds at once. We've been on the internet and our phones so long we've forgotten that there's a whole wide world out there. Life is supposed to be a bit risky now and then. Human existence used to be far more dangerous than it is today. Americans have spent years chasing comfort, ordering online, and watching Netflix. A lot of people have become boring, they don't try anything new, meet anyone new, join organizations, volunteer, or take risks. Their familiar bubble is where they live and venturing out of it causes anxiety. But the scariest thing for me is future regret, I don't want to look back at my life in my old age and leave anything undone. It's a big world, with food to eat, cultures to experience, and new people to meet. The world is waiting on you.

What's Normal?

When I was in Afghanistan during my first deployment it felt weird to see men constantly walking around holding hands with one another. In El Colacho in Spain once a year men dress up as yellow devils and jump over babies to protect them from evil spirits. In Lopburi in Thailand every year they have a monkey buffet ceremony for good luck, which is exactly what it sounds like. If you're not a Christian, then from an outside perspective taking the Holy Communion looks rather odd. Consuming the body and blood of Jesus? Moving abroad is going to redefine your normal. It's not for most people. This path is not for everyone, it can't be.

An unconventional life is for one kind of person, an unconventional person. In the United States we all live within the confines of a status quo bias, which adds levels of resistance to big changes like moving abroad. The majority of our neighbors are content going to the same restaurants and even ordering the same meal. Many of the people you know want to go to the same resort or vacation spot for decades at a time.

Throwing out the status quo and others' expectations can make for a messy affair. But for big changes to happen in your life, big changes have to happen. The thought *"what would other people think?"* holds a lot of us back from our dreams. Starting from scratch abroad isn't right or wrong. It's just different and people judge what's different. Be prepared for their self-righteous judgment, disapproval, questions, and pessimistic viewpoints. *Fuck'em.*

Beginning your new journey, check in on yourself to see how you're doing. Be gentle with yourself as you navigate your research, planning and execution of your new life. The first life you had wasn't perfect and your life overseas won't be either. But you're not limited by your past, and you can take forward what serves you and discard what doesn't. Moving abroad takes serious guts, and nobody said it was going to be easy. But worth it, yes. It might just be the best thing you ever did; it was for me.

Tips

- If you've never traveled internationally before, get some traveling experience before moving abroad.
- Don't expect life abroad to be like what it is at home.
- Your relationships will change.

Chapter 5

10 Moving Abroad Myths

There's a lot of misconceptions about moving abroad and a lot of information out there in the world, some good and some bad and some confusing. The reality is a lot of international travel rules change, especially when it comes to visas. Then every Veteran is unique, every individual and their situation varies. I'm going to answer some of the common myths about Veterans moving abroad to try to clear a few things up.

I'll lose my VA Compensation...

This is the most common one, a lot of Veterans are under the impression they need to reside in the United States to receive their VA compensation. However, the VA clearly states in its regulations that *"If you are a Veteran who lives overseas, you remain entitled to the benefits and services you earned through your military service."*[3] Essentially my friend, you aren't in the military anymore and they can't tell you where to live.

---

[3] https://www.benefits.va.gov/persona/veteran-abroad.asp

Your VA benefits are earned, not given and they can't just be taken away. In today's world you can do many of your VA appointments over the phone or computer. I like one of my doctors in the states and I still see him over video twice a year. I can get my medications, if necessary, through the Foreign Medical Program of the VA if its service connected or buy them over the counter cheap overseas. The VA will give you at least 90 days of your medications when you go abroad so you'll have time to figure out your medical situation.

The VA will not take your benefits from you if you decide to live abroad, there are some changes such as you're not eligible to participate in the VA Caregiver program. When you go back to the states, which you'll do occasionally you can still see the VA and do your appointments. I still do a yearly physical; I just schedule it when I'm going home to see my mom. It's good to stay connected to the VA, make sure you're getting your healthcare, medications and everything you need to be healthy abroad.

It's Not Safe Outside The United States...

We have this perception of the United States being safe and the world being dangerous. Lately I've felt as if the reverse is true as we see certain aspects of society decline. Morality and values aren't what they used to be - kids shoot up schools, drugs flow, and people commit terrible crimes. I feel a lot safer in the Dominican Republic or abroad than I do in the United States.

In American cities, there's this feeling that anything can happen at any time. And I mean anything, from a terrorist attack to a homeless person attacking you. That's not to say there isn't crime in the Dominican Republic, certain areas are very dangerous as they are in the states, but random crime is far less common.

In American cities there's this feeling that you have to be on guard all the time. If you're walking the street or going about your business, you have to keep both eyes open. For Veterans or anyone really, that's not a healthy way to live. You can't relax on a subway headed home after work, you have to keep an eye out for criminals and crazy people. Abroad most cities put a ton of emphasis on public transit safety, it's a top priority to keep people safe in those areas and protect transportation investments.

Veterans know how to take care of ourselves. We understand personal security, we can still read maps even if it's google maps we're doing our recon on. In every country there are precautions, I always wear zippers because I don't want to lose my shit, and I don't want to get pickpocketed. I pay attention in new cities, and I don't take drinks from strangers. In four years of living in the Dominican Republic, I've never had a safety issue. I've had plenty of people try to overcharge me for things sure, but that's a lot different than physical danger. Living abroad is far safer than most people assume.

Healthcare is inferior in other countries...

Despite having the most expensive healthcare system, the United States leads the world in chronic diseases, obesity and depression. Our homeland rarely comes to mind when you think healthy and happy. We have a serious crisis in our mental health, physical health and in our healthcare system.

Healthcare outside the United States is more affordable and in many ways it's superior. Many places throughout the world take Tricare, ChampVA, and treat veterans through the Foreign Medical Program of the VA for service-connected treatments. If you're retired, Tricare Overseasa exists throughout the world. If you're not, good news treatments and doctors are cheaper abroad. On top of that, medications can be pennies on the dollar compared to the United States. Many Veterans are surprised when they go abroad, and the same cholesterol medication is a fraction of the cost as it is in the states. Many medications are available over the counter without needing a prescription.

In the United States, often to get a simple medication is a complex process. There are doctors, insurance, pharmacists and hoops to jump through. Overseas oftentimes you can just pop into the corner pharmacy and get whatever you need for a couple bucks. Medical tourism outside the United States is booming because you can get surgeries and dental operations for half the cost. From hairline treatments to boob jobs to regular blood work tests, it's usually cheaper abroad.

You can live abroad for next to nothing...

Some veterans think you can move abroad and live off like $1,000 a month like a king. There are veterans in places like Eastern Europe, Vietnam, or Argentina that live off that amount. If you're American though it can be hard to go from always hot water to cold water, from electricity all the time to in and out lights and from drinking water out the tap to five-gallon jugs. It takes planning, effort and considerable sacrifice to live abroad for $1,500 a month or less.

That's one thing I tell Veterans when they move abroad, sure a local farmer in Thailand lives off $200 a month but you aren't a local Thai farmer bro. You're going to want more. A lot of Veterans get surprised when they realize a lot of first world luxuries still cost first world prices, especially in expat areas where things are higher. Every desirable country has certain cities or neighborhoods that are more Expat friendly than others. That's where you find the best infrastructure, restaurants, international schools and of course the highest prices. These higher cost areas also have the added benefit of being much safer than other areas of the country.

Living abroad isn't only about living cheaper; it's about living happier. It's not always about the cost, it's about what it's worth. Many expats end up spending around what they spend abroad as they did in the states but live a 100% better life.

Expat life isn't for veteran families...

Lots of families choose to leave the United States. Moving abroad with a family brings extra challenges but the quality of international private schools is often higher than US public schools. Plenty of families relocate abroad and there are lots of resources like Expat Child[4] that are geared towards family expat life. Military families are flexible and capable of living abroad and homeschooling is growing as a popular option.

There are additional challenges with moving abroad with a family but that also equals additional rewards. Your kids get a global education, develop independence and language skills. It's not the hippy, college kid sleeping in hostels type of life and there are still adult responsibilities. Kids adapt to change a lot easier than adults do and make friends easier. Kids throw temper tantrums and wake up

---

[4] https://expatchild.com/

in the middle of the night if you're in Barcelona or if you're in Boston.

Your kids and family are going to overcome challenges and get experiences abroad that your hometown can't offer. Kids can also help adults meet people and get integrated into the expat community because you'll meet people through their school. The kids' international school is going to be full of expats and those people will be there to help you transition and learn the tips and tricks of your area. Kids are always your best teachers and will help you more than you think on your expat journey.

Moving abroad will fix my problems...

You're still you no matter where you go. You can't outrun your problems. There will still be ups and downs in other countries and at times you'll be uncomfortable. It's a challenge to live abroad and can bring its own set of issues. For me, it was a big factor in my healing process. Our problems tend to follow us, but for myself and a lot of veterans moving abroad can provide a different perspective and peace. If you struggle with PTSD, moving abroad can make it better but it can also make it worse.

Unless you commit to a healing journey, moving abroad might not be the magic cure some Veteran think it will be. There's still work to be done, it's not a quick fix. There are some problems it might help with, if you've got family problems then space might be needed but you can't outrun the IRS or addiction, they'll always catch up to you. As Neil Gaiman writes, *"wherever we go, you take yourself with you."*

For some Veteran Expats, moving abroad doesn't solve problems and in fact creates new ones. Moving abroad splits your life into a before and after. You do have the opportunity to be a better person, but you can also slide into bad habits. There aren't necessarily the same roadblocks to your vices abroad, if I'm drinking a beer at 9 am in the Dominican Republic nobody looks twice.

I can't own property abroad…

In some countries you can and some you cannot. As a general rule, most countries allow foreigners to buy properties although with certain rules and restrictions. Many countries give Americans full property rights and in some those rights are nonexistent. Some countries make it very easy to buy property. It varies but be aware that these countries can also adjust their own real estate laws. It is true that you cannot use your VA home loan outside the United States and its territories.

You might want to buy a house where you can get more bang for your buck, or have less taxes. It's possible you're interested in getting an investment property abroad, which can be cheaper than in the United States. Foreigners can't own land in the Philippines or Thailand and in places like New Zealand you can't buy existing properties. In some countries, you can actually get your visa or citizenship through real estate investments and in some it makes no difference.

Financing properties abroad is often more complicated. You often need more money down, because there's nothing stopping you from getting on a plane and never coming back. Some U.S. banks will offer international home mortgages, like Citibank and HSBC. There is also developer financing, in the Dominican Republic where I live lots of developers offer flexible payment options.

I need to learn the language first...

When I moved to the Dominican Republic, I spoke zero Spanish. Now I'm halfway decent at it but you'll be surprised how much of the world speaks English. Lots of my military buddies abroad only speak English. In expat communities around the world many people get by with only English. Today's world of google translate, apps, and technology make the language aspect of moving abroad easier than ever.

Learning a language is occasionally easier than expats think, because fluency doesn't necessarily need to be the goal. If you move somewhere like Thailand, the language is very hard to learn and honestly nobody really expects you to learn it. However, learning a few key phrases, saying thank you in Thai and doing traditional greetings go a long way.

If you do want to learn the language, moving abroad is the best way to do it. There you'll be able to take formal classes, immerse yourself and hear it day to day. I never paid attention in high school Spanish but practical Spanish to me is easier. I might not be taking tests, but if I'm getting by in my community, ordering food, dealing with people, dating, communicating and all that good stuff then I'm doing pretty good. Once you do move or even commit to move, you're a hell of a lot more motivated to learn.

Living abroad is glamorous and exciting...

I wish every day was life at the beach or exploring fascinating cultures. But I still have to do my laundry, pay taxes, and deal with life's inevitable bullshit. You won't be on yachts every day popping champagne with beautiful people. Sometimes it can be messy and frustrating. It's still life - not a full-time vacation.

Sometimes it can be far less glamorous than Instagram suggests. People will post their curated photos of them at a beach club or laying in a hammock or surfing some beautiful wave. There's culture shock, language barriers, loneliness, homesickness and some people end up miserable. It's not the majestic paradise that a lot of Veterans might imagine and it's dangerous to over-romanticize it. That doesn't mean you don't get more luxury and bang for your buck, you absolutely do. But life is still life.

I hear it a lot, *"oh you're so lucky to live abroad."* Sometimes it feels that way and sometimes it doesn't. Usually I feel blessed and grateful, a lot more than I did in the states. I also do cooler shit. There are lots of misunderstandings and life abroad is often misrepresented on social media.

I can't own guns abroad...

This one is mainly true, for the most part at least. Nowhere on God's green earth is like the good ol' United States of Fuckin America when it comes to gun ownership. Gun ownership does vary country to country and many places around the world have outright bans. If you look at a map of the world of gun ownership, the United States would be bright green, the majority of the world would be yellow and some of the world would be red.

In America we have about five percent of the world's population but have almost fifty percent of the world's civilian guns. That's one reason nobody could ever invade America. The United States is the easiest and cheapest country in the world to buy and own guns, period. If you want to bring your guns with you abroad, it's not an easy task. It's usually best to sell your guns, gain residency in a gun friendly country and then buy guns using their system.

Concealed carry permits are very seldom issued abroad, in Bosnia you're good to go though. If moving to a gun friendly country is high on your list, be warned the license process is a lot different than what we're used to, guns are more expensive, and the process is lengthier. There are gun friendly countries out there, but most require background checks and a good reason to own a gun, such as sport shooting or hunting.

When Veterans talk about weapon importation, I usually tell them to not bother but if you want to subject yourself to international weapon shipping bureaucracy, go for it. Everywhere is going to have a hell of a lot more tape than the United States and many firearms and munitions that are legal to own at home will give you prison time abroad. The United States will not help you get out of jail abroad on a gun charge, or pay your legal fees or represent you in court if you get popped taking guns overseas or arrested.

Forward, March

Moving abroad can be challenging and lonely. But it can also be exciting and fun and at times yes, glamorous. There are a lot of misconceptions about moving abroad and some people who live abroad try to overly fantasize the whole thing. You see them on the beach, exploring cool places or editing videos to make everything look better. The social media influencer crowd sells their products as much as they sell their fake lifestyle. I never wanted to fall into this category, because I'm talking to Veterans. I'm speaking to my brothers and sisters, not some schmuck on the internet I want to waste money on a bullshit course or book a hotel through my site.

Reality comes for everyone abroad; you might distract yourself for a few months or even a year. But eventually you'll realize the glamor wears off and you'll be living your new normal. Living abroad initially means everything is new, exotic and you're curious about everything.

You don't have to be rich to live abroad, plenty of people living outside of America are middle class people but they are enjoying a high-class lifestyle. Moving abroad isn't perfect, but life isn't supposed to be perfect. The Veteran life is far from that, but Veterans can have a higher quality life abroad than in the United States for half the cost. You can afford to have a pool, or work out at the nice gyms, or hire a maid and go out to eat more.

One of the things that is luxurious to me is time. Moving abroad gives me more free time and that lets me write things like this, pursue my writing and creativity and basically spend my time how I want. Life abroad isn't sexy every second of every day, but it is an adventure.

Chapter 6

Lighten Your Load

How much shit do we need? I was packing up my apartment in Boston to head to the Dominican Republic and I could not believe how much junk I had. My possessions were put into four categories: garbage, sell, goodwill, or my keepsake box that I was mailing to my mom's house. I had more dead weight than I thought, and I bet you're in a similar position.

There's a quote from Tyler Durden played by Brad Pitt in *Fight Club* that *"the things you own end up owning you."* That resonated with me, and I discovered there's a certain simplicity and happiness with having less. The military taught me how little I actually needed to be happy, but I lost that when I resumed civilian life. Now I'm firmly in the camp of spending money on experiences, not things. You can have enough things, but you can never have enough experiences.

Possessions don't teach us anything, but you gain priceless life experiences and lessons through traveling. The older I get I realize that the excitement of buying new things fades fast but my memories live on. I'll never forget backpacking through Vietnam or being drunk singing beer songs at Oktoberfest in Munich. We've been taught, or maybe subconsciously trained, that more and more is the key to happiness when maybe the reverse is true.

When I finished downsizing my life, I had a couple of T-shirts left, my laptop, and not really much else. Technology helps us minimize; with a cellphone you have access to everything. I even tossed away all the extra cords we all collect and decided to go past mere possessions.

There were people in my life that didn't need to be in my future, if you're like me there are probably unnecessary people in your orbit as well. Once you start minimizing, you feel the benefits. We can't be true friends with all our Facebook friends, not everyone in your life deserves to be there just like not all of your possessions should make the move to your next life either. When you touch down in your new country, you'll want to be free of nonsense and that includes physical, mental and emotional baggage.

A lot of this happens naturally, you can't fit all your bullshit in your suitcase, so you have to leave some of it behind regardless. The people in your life who you don't make an effort to keep around, will drift away. Technology makes connections easier, and you'll want to prioritize the people who provide true friendship and value.

Adios

The only permanent goodbye in this life is death, wherever you go people can come visit and you can fly home when the homesickness hits or the holidays come around. You'll realize how much you were holding onto that really wasn't benefiting you. A lot of what you were carrying was weighing you down, mentally and spiritually.

Lightening your load is a weight off your soul. It's human nature to focus more on what you might lose than what you'll gain, but what if what you lose is to your advantage? When it comes to improving your life, a lot of people focus on what they need to do but sometimes it's better to think about what you need to let go. You need to let go of negativity, stress, addictions and pain.

Five Things to Leave Behind

- Yourself (at least the parts you don't like)
- Your Toxic Relationships
- Your Political Opinions
- Your Obsession with Time
- American Comparisons

Five Things to Pick up

- Local Relationships
- Expat Friendships

- Culture Skills
- A Fierce Curiosity
- Patience

The Case For Minimalism

We all seek a form of joy through possessions. Endless social media targeted advertisement bombards us and there's no escaping it. I'm a Chicago Bears fan because Chicago was the closest major city to where I grew up in smalltown Iowa. In case you're unaware, Iowa has no professional sports. When I moved to New York, I switched my Facebook Location to living in New York and the next day I was hit on my sidebar with shirts for Chicago Bears fans living in New York. Literally the outline of the state of NY with the Chicago Bears logo inside of it.

I bought the shirt and realized holy shit this advertising is effective. Americans work hard to get the big house, the new car, and the latest edition of the iPhone. Then turn around and spend money on vacations, not for the memories but for the Facebook photos. Our relationship with money has become unhealthy and we judge each other more based on dollar signs than character.

"Too many people spend money they haven't earned, to buy things they don't want, to impress people that they don't like."
~Will Rogers

Minimalism is a simpler life, but it doesn't equate to depriving yourself. It helps you rethink what adds real value to your life and what adds false value. Minimalism teaches a certain gratitude for the things you have, instead of a desire for what you don't. It's hard to kick the American mentality of keeping up with the Joneses. That doesn't mean doing the opposite and go so far that you don't enjoy material things. Extreme minimalism can be as stressful as over-consumerism.

Minimalism has become something of an art form in Eastern cultures where people have to live with less space. If your house has a walk-in closet, it compels you to fill it. If you take a glance through your wardrobe, I'd be willing to bet there are clothes you wear over and over and some that never see the light of day. Marie Kondo, author of *The life-changing Magic of Tidying Up* recommends a simple strategy, hold an item in your hands and ask yourself *"Does this spark joy?"* If the answer is no, then toss it.

I spent a year living out of a suitcase while traveling and that opened my eyes to a simple truth. Every item I purchased meant there was an item I had to get rid of. Buying a new T-shirt became a very serious thing, until I realized I was in Asia and each shirt cost around two dollars. Then I'd just buy a new tank top or two each week and donate the old ones.

Servicemembers turn into minimalists naturally, when you have to pick up and go all the time you don't collect as much. Everything you buy means something you have to move. When you know you have to move or deploy every few years, you're a little more cautious about what you buy. You learn it harshly on military missions, choosing what to take with you matters because every pound goes on your back.

You leave the bullshit behind because it's not like you can leave the gun and bullets. You get really careful with weight and space, military packing is an extreme sport. I don't own a car anymore, which means no registration fees, insurance, oil changes, car payment, and I don't have to deal with rising gas prices. This is your mission so take your mission essential items.

Public transportation is usually better and safer in other places and includes more options. In Thailand I can rent a scooter, I can hire a driver for the day somewhere, or I can use my god given two legs and walk places. I love taking the cable cars around Medellin in Colombia and I'm always impressed with subways in Asia, they run on time and are usually sparkling, eat off the floor type clean.

On my second expat journey living in the Dominican Republic, I arrived with less possessions than I've ever had. I realized I had everything I needed after I got my apartment. I could walk to the gym, the beach, and the store and I had my computer and an internet connection.

The beer was cold, and I figured out I could get my amazon packages delivered there too. Lightening your load is difficult but once you get going it feels better and better. Selling your stuff can be a good way to make extra cash as well before you move.

Starting Point

- If you have anything you haven't used or worn in six months- get rid of it.
- If you have multiples of things, two of basically the same shirt then you know what to do. How many coffee mugs do you need?
- Don't stress about what you paid for something, just because you dropped some cash on an item doesn't mean it has a forever place in your life.
- Think about if you lost this item or had it stolen, would you buy it again? If the answer is no, then you don't need it.

Your life isn't supposed to be a museum of your past experiences. My mother keeps things that she thinks other people might want years later. I don't see why anyone in the future would want to see my third-place soccer trophy from fourth grade. But she keeps it. Most of the things you own aren't priceless artifacts deserving of a permanent display case in your life. It's just stuff.

Take It Or Leave It?

When you move abroad, almost every time it's going to be cheaper to buy it there than ship it over. Especially when it comes to things like pots and pans, you'll learn it's pretty much all more affordable abroad. Having less things also is going to make it easier to move in the future, a lot of expats become serial expats and live in several different countries on their journeys.

Possessions over time are going to mean less and less to you as you live abroad. Happiness is composed of quality people and experiences, not things with price tags. Do your damnedest to minimize all of your snail mail before making the move abroad. Going paperless in today's world is easy and you can finally cancel that magazine subscription you've had for ten years.

You'll want to keep a US based address. My brother is kind enough to let me use his house in Iowa and my mail goes there and he keeps it for when I visit. I trust him and if you have a relative or close friend you trust I would do that. They can receive and kind of filter your mail for you. For example, the IRS still largely uses paper mail but most things you can digitize. This is your best option.

Your second, less preferable option would be to do a PO Box for your address which is going to be a hundred dollars a year or so depending on the size of your box and where it is. When you go back home to visit friends or family you can pick up your mail depending on how often you're planning on returning stateside.

Your third option is a digital mail forwarding service, a lot of younger digital nomads do this. They receive your mail at the business address, scan it and email it to you. As a veteran, I don't like the security risk of this and having someone have access to my information. I haven't used any of these companies, but I've talked to people who have utilized them successfully.

Mail Forwarding Services

- Ipostal1[5]
- PostScan Mail[6]
- Anytime Mailbox[7]

Your last option, one that I would not do but I'm making an attempt to be informative is to have USPS forward your mail internationally. You can fill out a change of address at the Post Office, just like you would do moving within the states and put in your international address. Many countries around the world don't have addresses like

---

[5] https://ipostal1.com/

[6] https://www.postscanmail.com/

[7] https://www.anytimemailbox.com/

you're used to in the states, they just don't exist in the same way.

If you're working for a reputable company abroad who has an address then maybe this would work for you, or if you're working a DoD job on a military base somewhere. For most expats I would say this is a dumb option and you'll never get your mail.

Packages

For packages and certain mail, you can use a mail forwarding service. This is what I do in the Dominican Republic and it's a common practice in many countries and expat communities. I use a service that has a physical location, they provide me an address in Florida to have packages sent to and they forward them over to the Dominican Republic.

There are some things I want that aren't available in the Dominican Republic, so I order them on Amazon. I also buy a lot of books because I don't like E-Readers. The company I use gives me an address in Miami and I have to pay weight between Miami and the Dominican Republic. They shoot me an email when I have a package waiting and I go pay a couple bucks and pick it up. Something heavy is costly and a book is a few dollars.

The only problem with this is that things over a certain price point can be heavily taxed and electronics are always taxed. I had a laptop break and ordered a new one, the laptop was $500 and to receive it I was taxed $200. I wasn't super happy but that's life. The service I use is called EPS[8] and you can look it up, but there are other comparable services in other countries. Expat blogs and message boards will have the best option for your area.

Letting Go

Having less things doesn't mean less happiness, or less satisfaction but it can mean more peace. Your possessions take your time from you, if you have something you're almost obligated to use it or spend time with it in some way. Like someone that buys a boat, you have to use it on your free weekends or what's the point of having it? A lot of us are guilty of buying some kitchen gadget only to use it once and away in a drawer it goes until we move.

You're absolutely not defined by your possessions, what kind of car you drive, or the square footage of your house. Your experiences, including your military service can never be taken from you but everything else can be.

---

[8] https://www.eps.com.do/en/

Chapter 7

From Dollars To Pesos

In traditional thinking, there are two ways of improving your financial situation. You can make more money, or you can spend less. Now there's a third option, you can just move abroad. I thought that being part of the mythical 1% would never happen to me, that's a club that would never grant someone like me entry. I grew up in Iowa with a single mother after my alcoholic, drug-addict father ran out.

My best friend growing up was an athlete but I was never going to dunk a basketball or hit a home run. He went to college on a football scholarship and played in the NFL, I skipped down the road to the local community college. That's when I discovered I liked booze and girls better than learning and before long I dropped out and strolled into the Army recruiting office.

Being rich was never something I considered and moving abroad widened my perspective to an interesting revelation. In order to be part of the top one percent of American earners, you need to make like $800,000 a year but that's America. As of this writing if you make over $60,000 you are part of the top 1% of global earners. When

I moved abroad, I thought maybe I wasn't poor, I was just in the wrong place.

Similar to that beer at the local store being a dollar, at the NFL game five dollars and at the fancy nightclub it's fifteen bucks. I was the same me, with the same money, I had just moved locations. That change in location changed everything because I catapulted from struggling in Boston to not worrying about bills in the Dominican Republic.

In the United States, it feels like money just flows through your fingers. Bills go up, taxes, and now there are hidden fees everywhere. Plus, everyone wants a tip all the time. You have to question whether going out to dinner and the movies is worth the cost. Moving abroad doesn't mean you never have to worry about bills, you're still living the human experiences and are going to have them. But what if you could throw whatever you wanted in the cart at the grocery store without worrying about the cost, what if you could afford to drink the good stuff and take those weekend trips?

Being a Veteran Expat provides unique financial advantages when you play it right. If you're on a fixed income, it provides a higher disposable income which means more of what you want and less of what you don't. It also can mean more free time and more money-saving opportunities, pay off your debt and investing in your future. More money always equals more opportunities.

$100 American dollars is current equivalent of:

Dominican Republic: 6,162.66 Dominican Pesos

Thailand: 3,350.40 Thai Baht

Costa Rica: 51,323.90 Costa Rican Colon

Philippines: 5,700.40 Philippine Pesos

Spain: 88.03 Euros

South Africa: 1,912.84 South African Rand

Vietnam: 2,575,750.00 Vietnamese Dong

Colombia: 432,207.40 Colombian Pesos

Mexico: 2,028.70 Mexican Pesos

Indonesia: 1,674,281.41 Indonesian Rupiahs

The current weakest currency in the world is either the Lebanese Pound or the Iranian Rial. I doubt you'll be gung-ho to move to those countries but understanding currencies, conversion rates and money transfers are an important aspect of Veteran expat life.

Going Back In Time

I was born in 1986 and the median rent in the United States at that time was a whopping $432 a month. Unfortunately, there's no time machines in either DeLorean's, hot tubs or anywhere else I'm aware of so we have to make the best of the moment. Finding a great place for that $432 a month out there in the world though is very doable.

We all might want to live in mansions off the coast of Greece, on Martha's Vineyard or own a personal island but for most of us that ain't happening. What you can have is a higher quality life abroad at a fraction of the cost of what it would take in the states. Moving abroad can feel like going back in time because you can have those 1986 prices at nice dinners, taxi rides and nightlife.

Let's Talk Money

There's no successful Veteran expat journey without a successful financial story. In America it's a lot easier to talk about sex, politics and religion than it is our finances. We'll talk about the most offensive things but talking about someone's personal finances is off-limits.

The costs of moving abroad add up quick and hidden costs and unexpected expenses are always there. With a forward-thinking strategy you can minimize some of these costs and eliminate financial missteps. Spending the necessary cash probably isn't going to bother you but you don't want to waste money.

A lot of first-time Veteran expats squander their hard-earned money during the initial move and first year abroad with costly blunders. There's lots of misinformation out there on the financial aspect of overseas life. I wouldn't completely rely on one source, because lots of things change in markets, real estate and currencies.

There are two sides to every country and your mission is to operate in the space between them as an expat. You have a tourist side and then an everyday life side, the prices are far different between these two categories. Same as you can rent an apartment in your American city for cheaper monthly than you can live in a hotel. Then there are pricier restaurants you head to on special occasions and some you'll go to every day.

The prices can be far different in the same city, locals in Cancun aren't paying what tourists are paying. Money problems are often failure point for Veteran expats, they can't figure out how to manage their money abroad and transition from vacation type spending to normal life. Plus being broke anywhere sucks, even in paradise.

Chapter 8

Cost Of Living

How much does it cost to live abroad? How much does it cost to live in the Dominican Republic? Thailand? Brazil? Portugal? This is the most common question I get from Veterans.

It's also an impossible question to answer without knowing more information or the person. How much does it cost to live in your city? It ranges from a lot to a little around the world.

I think what a lot of them are trying to ask, is *"How little do I need to live there?"* Which again, is hard to answer because everyone has a different ideal lifestyle abroad. My city in the Dominican Republic has villa rentals for $3,000 a month and studio apartments for $300 a month. You most likely want to be in between those two numbers but your spending habits are going to be unique to you. Can you leave cheaper abroad? Of course, but you can also spend more. I've done both.

I have a Marine friend who lives in the same town that I do in the Dominican Republic. He's a Marine so I think he just likes hardship or something and he spends less than half of what I do every month. He's very frugal, doesn't drink alcohol and lives in an apartment that I would never live in. I go out to eat all the time, drink the good stuff and live in a sweet ass condo.

This Marine doesn't own a vehicle; I own a golf cart. His hobbies are going to the gym and the beach, and my hobbies are scuba diving and golf. We live a mile away from each other and are both Veterans and live drastically different financial lives. He's also probably one of the happiest people that I know, but I know I personally wouldn't be happy with his lifestyle.

When it comes to analyzing your potential financial expenses from one place to another there are two tools that are somewhat similar in application. A cost-of-living index and a cost-of-living calculator. The cost-of-living index is broader and compares basic costs such as housing, childcare, gas and more year over year. The calculator is a tool using the index data to help you estimate how much you'll need to live in a specific location. The index is generalized data, such as the cost of living in Punta Cana and the calculator is what you would use to input your data to see what your life might be there.

The Math

Veterans and people on social security receive cost of living adjustments, such as our VA benefits going up over time because of cost-of-living index data rising. This cost-of-living adjustment or COLA is based around inflation rates. Which from an economic standpoint means it's not great when we get a bump in Veteran compensation or SSDI or social security because it means that the cost of living has also increased.

Those numbers are calculated generally for Veterans across the entire country because $500 buys a lot more goods and services where I'm from in Iowa than New York City. The U.S. Bureau of Labor Statistics does publish the Consumer Price Index[9], which is useful economic data but that isn't a cost-of-living index. The government doesn't provide a cost-of-living index but instead analyzes a broad range of data to calculate adjustments for things like the military's Basic Allowance for Housing rate changes.

It's important to consider your personal long-term plans and goals when you're thinking about your cost of living abroad. Maybe you want to aim to save a certain percentage of your income monthly or you have long term bills like child support or need to pay for a kid's car or education. You could have aging parents and need to think about how that expense might manifest in years to come, you want to ensure no matter where you choose to

---

[9] https://www.bls.gov/cpi/

live that you'll be able to save money monthly and year over year.

A cost-of-living calculator is a valuable tool to help you analyze costs and compare the expenses of one places versus another. It'll help you compare where you are to where you want to be and help you make better informed decisions. You shouldn't just straight out rely on this data; it doesn't take in human decisions or how you'll spend in your new environment.

We all have certain necessary expenses such as food and housing, then we have our discretionary spending and personal habits. Some Veterans love a Friday night at home eating Ramen noodles, and some are going to want to hit the fancy restaurant with a hot date. I'm more in the latter category.

The Big Three: Housing, Transportation and Food

The largest bill we have in the United States for your average American is housing. But housing isn't just housing, it's maintenance, upgrades, taxes and household bills. Most financial experts will tell you to spend 30% or less of your income on housing. In practical terms, if your income is going to be $4,500 per month in Costa Rica then you want to pay less than or at $1,350 on your rental. I'd recommend not going above 25% of your income on rent.

Transportation is the second biggest thing that eats up our dollars in the United States. Americans spend around 17% of our income on transportation related costs. One thing I love about being abroad is transportation is generally cheaper because not everyone owns a vehicle. Our country, in most areas at least it's very much a necessity to own a car. Some of its climate related, you can't drive a little scooter in upstate New York, but you can ride a scooter year-round in the Dominican Republic. As you might imagine, scooter expenses are cheaper than cars.

Many cities have great public transportation because the population heavily relies on it to get around. Everything from subways to taxis are remarkably more affordable and available for the day-to-day person in cities abroad. Besides that, many expat areas are far more walkable than American cities.

Where I live, I don't own a car, but I do have a golf cart. I mainly have that for fun though, I bought it on a whim, and I don't rely on it for transportation. I can walk from my apartment to the gym, stores, bars, the beach and restaurants and I don't need to go many more places than that most days. You can ship your car abroad, though it's rarely worth it. You can rent a car abroad sometimes cheaper than renting one.

When it comes to food costs abroad it varies quite a bit. A lot of Veterans who go abroad are surprised at the cost of food and that's because they want to eat the same stuff as in the states. Local food costs local prices imported food costs a lot more. When you eat what the locals eat, you'll eat much cheaper. Sometimes this takes a little bit of courage for us, and you might be looking around for restaurant health certificates that don't exist in certain countries.

I've gotten sick a few times, once pretty bad in Vietnam eating street food but you get through it and learn. If you made it through the military, you should have a stronger stomach than the average person. Drink the local beer and not the Guinness or Corona and it'll be a lot cheaper. Ask locals for recommendations, ask where they eat and where they grocery shop and go hunt those places down. Skip the Whole Foods type grocery store in the expat neighborhood for most purchases.

I'm talking about the Big 3 because those are the most important categories to reduce when going abroad and you should look for ways to save. If you're a Veteran on a fixed income you should set yourself up to spend less in these categories in your new country. A lot of good apartments are on public transportation lines and if you live walking distance of necessities you'll save a lot of money.

Best Cost of Living Calculators

- Numbeo[10]
- Expatistan[11]
- Livingcost[12]

Some costs in today's technology economy are standardized across the board. I'm paying the same for Netflix, Spotify and other similar things no matter where I'm living. Then a few costs go up when I move abroad, like my cellphone since I pay for an unlimited international plan. Even some costs like my vitamins and the protein oatmeal I like cost more because I have to pay extra for shipping for my Amazon stuff in the Dominican Republic.

The bourbon I drink costs more because it has to be imported from the United States, so the idea that everything is cheaper across the board is false. Electronics are one item that can be more expensive or cheaper depending on where you're at in the world. As you can imagine, things like clothes and technology items are significantly cheaper in Asia.

---

[10] https://www.numbeo.com/cost-of-living/

[11] https://www.expatistan.com/cost-of-living

[12] https://livingcost.org/

Costs of moving abroad

- Your plane ticket
- Visas and immigration fees
- Storage units stateside
- Initial move-in costs, security deposits, and bullshit fees
- Shipping your stuff
- Transferring cash, ATMs, financial aspects
- Furnishing your new place
- Unexpected expenses

Some people think of the cost of living abroad and forget it costs money to get there. Usually, you'll also need a return ticket unless you've already got dual citizenship or have your visa figured out. The United States usually wants to make sure you have one, so the airline usually will ask. Every time I fly back to the Dominican Republic, I have one, then just cancel or adjust the date for a few months later. You're always going to get hit with unexpected fees when you first get to your new country.

You will always spend more money when you're new in a place and you have to plan for that. Once you connect with locals and make some expat friends, you'll figure out ways to save. You'll want to make friends and ask people references or who you should hire for any maintenance, lawn services, maids, mechanics and the like. It's a new environment, you don't speak the language and it's easy to get overcharged. Your personal cost of living will go down over time as you settle in, stop splurging and get your finances figured out.

Minimal Living Cost

This is something everyone should calculate but especially before moving abroad and again when you get abroad. Minimal Living Cost is the bare essentials of how much you need to survive. When you do this accurately, you'll be amazed at the unnecessary things we spend money on from expensive coffee to subscriptions to new clothes.

- Rent
- Groceries
- Bills (cell phone, electricity, internet, etc.)
- Transportation
- Anything you place in the "Would die without category"

When you arrive at your calculation, then check to see how much you spent last month there's no way those numbers are going to be the same. I'm not saying they should be the same, we should enjoy ourselves but it's a clear look at your unnecessary expenses. Veterans deserve luxuries in my opinion but everyday can't be balling out or bottomless mimosas.

Finances are something we have to take a harder look at moving and living abroad because we might not have the same safety nets. Double check all your numbers, use resources and be honest with yourself about money. It's easy to blow through money abroad, especially when you're looking at foreign currencies like monopoly money.

Chapter 9

The Financial Planning

Before you hop on that plane, you have to get your finances in order. This might mean taking time to pay off debt, figuring out banking, addresses, credit cards, taxes and handling investments. If you get this right, most of the other things will fall into place but if you fuck it up, financial stress abroad can be worse than in the states.

I've seen Veteran expats even get stuck abroad and not be able to afford a plane ticket home after a medical emergency, blowing their money on something stupid, or losing access to their money. Sometimes when you don't have as much to do on your schedule, it's easy to find yourself spending more money.

I talk to veterans planning their moves five years out and the earlier you get started the better. Plan a realistic financial timeline and meticulously dive into your finances. There are lots of free resources out there when it comes to financial planning and Veterans should take better advantage of them. Especially when it comes to moving abroad, you should be diving into your budgeting, spending and investments to ensure you succeed in this next chapter.

You can meet with a professional or do it with free resources or do it on your own. The most important thing is that you do it and plan your move abroad with the serious financial consideration it deserves. It's important you take the time and sit down with a paper and pen to actually drill down your finances, expenses abroad and in the states before and after you move abroad.

Net Worth

Calculating your net worth can be a painful and sobering exercise but it's the first thing you need to do. Your net worth is all of your assets, cash, 401ks, real estate and such then subtract your liabilities like student loans and credit card debt.

As a veteran, you understand sacrifice and you should start saving now to thrive later. If you're planning on looking for work once you get to your new country, have as much as you can to live off during the time it takes you to get a job.

Net Worth Resources

• Ramsey Solutions Net Worth Calculator[13]

---

[13] https://www.ramseysolutions.com/

- Bank Rate's Net Worth Calculator[14]
- AARP's Net Worth Calculator[15]

Tracking

Where the fuck is my money going? I was shocked to discover how much I was spending on things like food, booze, and my car. Not tracking where your money is going is one of the biggest financial mistakes people can make. The simplest way to cut real spending is to examine the Big 3: *Housing, Transportation, and Food.* Cut costs in these three areas first to get the most bang for your buck to plan your Veteran expat move.

We have a consumerism driven culture in America and breaking free of that is a complicated process. Break that habit before you go abroad and axe your overspending. You'll find when you're doing your financial planning to go abroad, you won't want to go out and blow cash on stupid things. You'll want to save your money for experiences, good times and daily life in your new country.

No matter where your current budget is, even if you're dead broke at the moment that doesn't mean moving

---

[14] https://www.bankrate.com/smart-spending/personal-net-worth-calculator/

[15] https://www.aarp.org/

abroad is impossible. It might take a few months or even years of planning, that's what big goals often require - sacrifice and time. If moving abroad is your dream, then join the Peace Corp on a two-year contract and go work in another country. You can look into something like Wwoofing[16] (Worldwide opportunities on Organic Farms) which is farmwork abroad.

There's also nothing wrong with waiting a bit, I talk to people every day who are waiting until retirement, their pension kicks in or maybe the kids leave the house. These people are usually successful Veteran expats because they plan their exit strategy and don't give into the temptation of being impulsive. If you're a former servicemember, you know the value of planning and oven overplanning. I don't think there's anything wrong with occasionally winging it but not when it comes to money.

Timeline

Even if the desire to buy a one-way ticket to Mexico or a beach somewhere feels overwhelmingly strong, think about a targeted date first. Most Veterans I talk to already have a date in mind. For some it's when they hit their twenty years in the military and are retiring abroad. Other veterans are waiting for their kids to get out of the house

---

[16] https://wwoof.net/

or waiting on a second retirement. It's easier than ever to move out the United States whether it's a permanent thing, a couple months sabbatical or an extended vacation.

VA Benefits Abroad

Veterans often thrive as expats because we've got something most people don't and that's our military benefits. Lots of us get that regular VA compensation on the first of every month and that opens up the world. If you get your retirement plus your VA benefits, you've got it made in the shade. If you don't, there are plenty of places where you can live well off your VA benefits. Not many other expats have what we have, but not many people stepped up, sacrificed and went through the fire.

The VA benefits I was getting gave me a lot more confidence than others to take the leap. I took the leap abroad because I knew I could make it abroad after I figured out the recipe and lifestyle, the VA benefits gave me a cushion and enabled me to chase my dreams. My dream was to write, I wanted to be a writer and now I can say I'm doing it. If I can write part time and adventure part time and party part time then I'm a happy Veteran.

Back Home Maintenance Costs

Moving abroad shouldn't be a half measure and unless you're wealthy I doubt you want to maintain two different residences and sets of bills. Paying rent for somewhere you're not living can feel dumb after a while. But you should have a place to return to when you do your trial run, don't take a weeklong vacation and just sell your house.

Some things are unavoidable, your debt will follow you wherever you go. Child support, college loans, taxes, and certain types of expenditures are usually inescapable no matter how off the grid you get. A lot of Veterans when planning their move abroad forget about all the small things, go through your bank statements to see your subscriptions from the gym to HBO.

Storage

Look at every single item you need to store closely and if you aren't sure, that's a sign to get rid of it. If you can sell it, then sell it. If you can see yourself storing it for five years without touching it then donate it. Take with you what you absolutely MUST have and store the rest. Don't throw away your keepsakes or sentimental items, but if you can avoid storage costs you should do it. If you can't, then research a storage unit that is going to work within your budget and try to pay it up front to get a deal. Or best case scenario, store your important belongings with a relative.

I know Veterans that pay thousands of dollars to store things in the states they'll probably never wear, use or drive again. A lot of us find it hard to get rid of certain possessions but then you'll still have that nagging bill in the United States every month.

Take The Leap

A lot of people go right up to the edge of moving abroad and don't pull the trigger. They are almost people but Veterans are far from almost people. We did join the military, we didn't almost join. There's a lot of people exploring the idea of moving abroad, reading blogs, watching YouTube and TikTok but few are going to execute.

Money makes everything easier and the more you have of it, the simpler the move and life abroad will be. It's not going to be easy no matter what, but the more reliable income you have the better your life overseas is going to be. Maybe money can't buy happiness, or maybe it can but it can buy freedom. Freedom to me equals happiness, freedom to spend my days how I want, freedom to not worry about alarm clocks and not worry about other people's opinions.

Chapter 10

Gringo Prices

Gringo prices in Latin America and what's referred to as Farang prices in Thailand are a reality of expat life especially when you're first getting started. You're going to resemble a dollar sign more than a person to some locals overseas. Your financial situation is going to transition from a more formal economy in the United States to an informal economy abroad. That informal economy can be difficult to navigate when you first get there.

You're going to be in a world without price tags and it's a financial culture shock. It's a tug of war where they want you to pay as much as possible for a good or a service and you want to pay as little as possible. In your life now you'll have to say the dreaded *"How much?"* question more than you'd like. You'll likely be offended here and there when people try to significantly upcharge you.

Some battles aren't worth fighting, some are. In certain areas, prices are just generally inflated like Cancun in Mexico or Punta Cana in the Dominican Republic or Jaco in Costa Rica. Because that's where the tourism and money is. Often times the best thing to do is just walk away because you never need to buy anything.

Quick Tips

- Speaking the language, or at least a little bit, is going to help you a lot with prices.
- You'll want to agree on a price before getting into a taxi if there's no meter.
- Don't make anyone lose face.
- Be respectful, even when someone is trying to take advantage of you.
- Negotiating is an integral part of many cultures.

The gringo price is more of a problem for the first few months moving abroad. Because they don't know that you're not a tourist and it takes time to develop relationships. This adjustment phase can leave a lot of expats frustrated when they initially move abroad. Once you are somewhere for a while, you'll know what things should cost, you'll have a regular taxi driver, and you'll know where to shop. People will test you, just to see if you'll pay the first price they quote you.

Don't take people trying to rip you off personally. You also shouldn't assume everyone is trying to rip you off, a beer on the beach costs more than a beer at the store. Every area is going to have different negotiating dos and don'ts. When you walk into a store to buy something, you should know another store is going to sell that too. When I was buying a stove in the Dominican Republic, I just went to three stores and compared the prices. When you take the time to do that, you'll buy with more confidence.

I was on a date once in the Dominican Republic and I was trying to buy a t-shirt and the girl I was with was incredibly furious at the shopkeeper. It was a funny reality show to me because I would ask the price for a shirt, and they'd quote me some outrageous amount and she would yell at them. I started asking the shopkeepers how much stuff was just to see her reaction when they told me. Then I realized if I liked something, I could just have her go in and buy it for half the price that I could. It made for a fun social experiment and date, but it highlighted the economic differences between us. Blending in is a good way to avoid gringo prices but there's no blending in some places.

The Barter Economy

The best advice I can give you on bartering overseas is that if you don't like the price, don't buy it. It's kind of as simple as that because whatever item you're haggling over is worth how much you're willing to pay for it. When my mom visited me in Asia, she had never bartered with anyone, and she wanted to buy some of the knockoff goods at a night market. She kept just taking the first price she was quoted, and it was driving me a bit crazy. The sellers were surprised because as a general rule nobody takes the first price.

Finally, I convinced her that she had to barter on the next item and when the guy quoted her a price on a purse, she offered him 5% less than the guy was asking for and the merchant of course quickly agreed. She felt like she was wheeling and dealing like a local, so I let her have that win but come on mom. Haggling is a normal part of a lot of cultures and informal economies.

If the first price a seller tells me is insane, I'll usually just move on. If they are just trying to rip me off then I don't want to support that business. If something is a touch higher than what it should be, I'll usually just buy it. If something should cost me 200 pesos and they charge me 250, I'm not too concerned. Expats hyper focusing on money is not a good way to live and you'll meet expats like this that just want the cheapest possible everything.

On a recent trip to Jamaica, I was with a group of people on a tour and afterwards we all went out for a few drinks together after horseback riding. It was a great day and one of the girls was staying in a hotel near mine, so we decided to split a taxi on the way back. We knew about what it should cost, and the guy was insanely overcharging us for a five-minute taxi ride. A good thing about Jamaica is that they speak English, and this Canadian girl said to him, *"How about you be a man of Christ and just give us a fair price on this ride?"* He dropped his price, and I'll remember that line for the rest of my life.

Chapter 11

Working Abroad

No clear model exists when it comes time for finding work abroad. Every person's skills, education, and financial needs are going to be different. There are a lot of jobs abroad that, frankly, just don't pay enough to be worth doing. Sometimes working is about being productive, positively occupying your time, or enjoying yourself rather than just making money. But there's no denying we live in the real world and all have bills to pay, sometimes working abroad is a necessity and sometimes it's a luxury and sometimes it's a passion.

A lot of Veterans want to make money online or be digital nomads. We all imagine the dream life of working online and making tens of thousands of dollars a month. Most people that claim that on social media are lying to you, it's smoke and mirrors to get you to buy something or watch something. Everyone has a much different skill set and background and many of those don't translate to the technological world.

I was in the infantry; they did not prepare me to make money coding or writing software or any cyber skills whatsoever. So, when Veterans tell me they want to make money online, I'm not sure if they want to start an Onlyfans, sell crypto, or do something that they know how to do. There's no magical making money online formula but if I figure one out, I'll be the first to let you know.

The best model for living a higher quality life abroad as an American is to earn dollars and spend in a weaker currency. It's the ideal situation, if you have a pension, it's the same deal. It's going to be easier for you to save money if you've got a location independent job. I can write from anywhere in the world although it's not like I'm making tons of money doing this.

We live in a digital age and there's a lot of remote work, if you're already working remotely then you're a good candidate to move abroad. Working remotely is easy for some people and difficult for others, if you have skills in that area then it's simpler. If you are technologically illiterate, then it's going to be more of a challenge for you to find remote work.

The most common jobs I see expats working are teaching English, running restaurants and bars, or real estate. If you have some form of professional skills that the world needs, most of them will transfer abroad. Everyone wants medical professionals, engineers, and useful people.

Get creative when thinking about working abroad. I meet divemaster's, yoga instructors, chefs, social media influencers, musicians, personal trainers, and acupuncturists abroad. Nobody really needs someone who is just a bartender, with the exception if they need someone that speaks multiple languages or maybe you're just so beautiful it'll reel customers in. Whatever field you're in, is there a way to do it remotely? Some jobs the answer is yes and some it's going to be a hard no.

The taxes of money earned abroad can be complicated and differ from country to country. If you take up residency in certain countries, all your worldwide income is subject to their taxation. Other nations only will tax your local income, or income earned within their borders. Usually a foreign retirement check or disability compensation will be untaxed by the local government.

It's up to you to check, certain places abroad are a more informal economy, and it can be hard to figure out the right thing. You'll want to be careful, sometimes being double taxed is a part of working abroad and sometimes not. Hopefully in the future less and less double taxing will occur.

Unskilled jobs or laborers don't transfer abroad because someone is going to be willing to do them cheaper. If you're planning on doing road work, driving trucks or construction abroad it's going to be difficult unless you do it through a US based company. If you want one-on-one work like being a personal trainer, just like in the states it takes building up a clientele. Most expat personal trainers

I see don't make a ton of money unless they sell subscriptions or programs online or effectively utilize social media.

To a lot of people moving abroad without a job seems like an absurd idea, but it's much easier to find a job in your ideal country if you're already there. Finding a job in a certain country is a lot harder if you're not already there or have significant connections. If you have a dream of living in Brazil or Germany, then moving there and then looking for work is an option if you've got the guts for it.

You can find opportunities in your new country far easier, interview in person, and they're more likely to view you as a serious candidate if you're already there. One reason I talk to Veterans about moving abroad and we make good expat candidates is that we already have a guaranteed income from our benefits or retirement.

Government jobs

A lot of expats and former military personnel like us might work government or contracting jobs overseas. With the Department of Defense (DoD), State Department, United States Agency for International Development (USAID), or other employment. You want to keep that government years coming if you got out of the military short of your twenty year mark. Or maybe you want to work towards that coveted second retirement. Working for the government abroad provides a lot of options and benefits and some drawbacks because you know, it's the government.

Gov Job Links

- ClearanceJobs[17]
- GoGovernment.org[18]
- FederalJobs.Net[19]
- USAjobs[20]
- Then there is your normal job listing sites like ZipRecruiter, Indeed, etc.

Applying for a government job overseas can provide meaningful employment where you can make a difference in a field that you're passionate about. It can expose you to different countries while still having a connection to the United States. Then you get government assistance and a more streamlined process to work visas and things opposed to going at it solo. You'll have an obvious advantage in this field if you can speak a second or third language. If you have military service, you'll also get job preference in overseas government work.

---

[17] https://www.clearancejobs.com/

[18] https://gogovernment.org/

[19] https://federaljobs.net/

[20] https://www.usajobs.gov/

Multinational Orgs

Multilateral Organizations are when three or more countries form an organization to pursue a common interest or goal. There are people out there who think these organizations do a lot for the world and people who believe they do little. I had the opportunity to work in partnership with the United Nations in Afghanistan where I thought they were impeding progress. Then I saw the United Nations in Africa and thought they were doing a good job, so with any organization and bureaucracy there are going to be pros and cons.

I wouldn't necessarily write an organization off or be gung-ho to join it because of what you've previously heard. Here are some examples of the larger multilateral organizations and they're always going to be hiring and always posting jobs through their official channels.

- United Nations
- NATO
- World Bank
- World Health Organization
- Unicef
- International Criminal Court

Remote Working Abroad

With the explosion of remote work, lots of people are choosing to live overseas. If you're already working from your computer, then going overseas is simpler. Many jobs transitioned to remote work during the pandemic, and some went back to in-person. I'd like for us to go back to all hanging in nature and eating fruit with no phones, but I don't think it's happening.

If you've got digital skills, then you're ahead of the game and if you don't it might be time to *"Learn to code"* or something. If you're a nerd, you might as well monetize that knowledge to earn your financial freedom. It's a challenge to sift through all the nonsense when it comes to looking for remote work. First think about your skills and experience then apply them to earn a remote income. When you google remote work a lot of garbage will come back but there might be a diamond hiding in it.

You can spend years reading about *"making money online"* or similar topics. When I wrote the second edition of this book, I reached out to job recruiters, posted on message boards and tried to find ways to connect Veterans to solid remote employment. It didn't pan out and I'd rather provide less advice than bad advice or promote scams. I'm sure there are great recruiters out there for online work, but they are generally field or skill specific. There's not any universal guidance that would apply to every Veteran when it comes to working abroad.

Check Some Sites

- SideHustleNation[21] - To find a side hustle.
- Flippa[22] – Buy and Sell online businesses, ecommerce, etc
- SmartPassiveIncome[23] - Networking, they have free and paid options.
- Latonas[24] – Selling online businesses

Benefits of Remote Work

- No Commute Stress
- Better Work-Life Balance
- Financial Savings

Drawbacks of Remote Work

- Networking is Much More Challenging
- It Can Get Lonely
- It's Not For Everyone

---

[21] https://www.sidehustlenation.com/

[22] https://flippa.com/

[23] https://www.smartpassiveincome.com/

[24] https://latonas.com/

Examples of Virtual Jobs

- Web Designer
- Systems Analyst
- Programmer
- Online Teacher
- Personal Coaching
- Online Entrepreneur
- Software Jobs
- Freelancer
- E-Commerce
- Video Editing
- Virtual Coaching
- Stock Trading
- Human Resources
- Virtual Assistant
- Vlogger
- Social Media Management
- Teaching Online
- Stock/Crypto Traders
- Artist
- Online Sales

Tourism Jobs

- Cruise Ship Employment
- Scuba Instructor • Hostel Employee
- Bartending
- Ski Instructor

- Fitness Trainer

Abroad Tip: *You'll want to tailor your resume based on the country you're in. American resumes can have a different structure than other countries. There are lots of jobs in the tourism field abroad based on your skills, passions, and experiences.*

Explore Remote Work Options

- FlexJobs
- RemoteJobs
- Remote.com
- We Work Remotely
- No Desk
- LinkedIn Remote Jobs
- Working Nomads
- Just Remote
- JobSpresso
- List of Established Remote Companies

If working remotely is your goal, specify on your resume that's what you're looking for when applying. You can write *"Location independent"* on your resume or application. You want to show why you can work abroad because it requires more responsibility and discipline than traditional office roles. You'll probably need to understand and be effective in working with collaboration tools, which is like Slack, Microsoft Teams, Zoom, etc. You must be comfortable with technology.

Note: *Other terms for remote work can include Distributed Workforce, Work From Home, Work From Anywhere and Virtual Job.*

Remote work attracts a lot of scams, so you'll need to be careful in your search. Product testing is usually a scam and so are things like secret shopping. Nobody is going to pay you to just buy things online. A red flag is if the job requires up front expenses by you, if you're unsure you can look the company up on the Better Business Bureau and the Federal Trade Commission. I've met Veterans who've gotten scammed out of things online while searching for ways to make additional income, if something seems too good to be true, it usually is.

Consider Passive Income

There's not really such thing as passive income. I'd like to think we could just sit around and have all this money flowing to us but it's not that easy. Maybe there's people that will tell you that you can, I don't know how though. I view my military retirement now as a source of passive income, but it's not like I didn't do a lot to earn it. Having this steady income allowed me to deviate from what I'll call *"normal life"* and live life more on my terms.

My books are a form of passive income and so are things like rental properties that don't involve everyday effort. Time is the most valuable resource we have. Putting in the upfront work can pay dividends later on and that's part of the moving abroad planning. I have a friend who's a veteran and a musician in the Dominican Republic and every ninety days he gets a royalty check and that enables him to live a high-quality life on top of his military benefits. It might take some creativity on your part, investigation and hard work to develop remote income but every dollar helps and every dollar goes further abroad.

Ideas For Passive Income

- Rental Properties
- Digital Products
- Dropshipping
- Financial Investments
- Online Courses
- Create An App
- Write A Book
- Social Media Sponsorships
- Sell Designs/Photos Online
- Annuities
- Business Investments
- CDs
- Rent Something
- Blog
- YouTube Channel
- Art Investments

Pretty much any attempt at earning passive income is going to require some kind of work or investment up front. Even if you're putting something you own to work for you, like renting out a car, it still requires effort on your part. In today's world it can feel like you need multiple income streams to be successful and if you can find ways to make a few extra bucks a month you should do it.

Every veteran has different skills and goals when it comes to earning money abroad. Most local jobs aren't going to pay you enough to be worth doing unless you have some special skill or don't need the money. Lots of Veterans look for unique ways to supplement their income. An amazing thing I've noticed is how many veterans living abroad volunteer their time and energy to help out local populations and fellow veterans.

When you get abroad, you'll see business opportunities around you. You'll network with people who are working online or in your new country and doors will open up. You'll notice your town doesn't have or needs something that you can provide, you'll see where you can add value. When you start to look around, you'll be amazed at the kind of things you'll see and range of possibilities.

Chapter 12

Veteran Healthcare Abroad

———————◈———————

Healthcare is usually the top concern Veterans have when moving abroad. In America we're stuck on the idea we've got the best healthcare in the world but if that was the case we wouldn't be so fat, sick and depressed. We lead the world in chronic diseases and if you've walked into a Walmart lately, I'm sure you've taken a look around and thought, *"Something's gone terribly wrong."*

We overthink healthcare because we've built ourselves an overcomplicated system and navigating it is like a *Lord of the Rings* quest. There's no reason to think you'd need more healthcare abroad; in fact, it'll probably be less. You might be pleasantly surprised how happier and healthier you feel, both mentally and physically overseas.

Outside of the United States, other countries attempt to design their systems to be more understood and deliver an affordable service. It's common knowledge that the United States is one of the best countries if you're seriously ill, with something like cancer. In that regard, we're the envy of the world with the best equipment, doctors and medicines. If you don't fall into that category, you can often get superior healthcare abroad.

When you start googling options for healthcare abroad you might be more confused than before you started your research. Some of that's intentional, because then it becomes easier to sell you something. Sort of like fitness programs that make working out so complicated that you need to buy their system when in reality you need to eat healthier and exercise more.

The healthcare I've received outside the United States, both through the Veterans Administration and privately has been superior to what I've gotten at clinics at home. Most importantly, it's a hell of a lot cheaper. You'll be shocked to discover things can literally be one tenth of the price as in the states when it comes to things like medication. From dental cleanings to cholesterol medication to Brazilian butt lifts, it all costs less. When the costs are lower, it provides more peace of mind because you don't have that feeling like you can't afford to be sick or get seen.

No Rush

Most of the time, pretty much all of the time it makes more sense to get your healthcare set up when you get to your new country, not before. To a lot of Veterans that might seem counterproductive or worrisome, it's not. If you feel the unstoppable need for temporary insurance, then look up a reputable travel insurance company until you get settled.

You can talk to other expats and see what they're using and evaluate your life and needs. A lot of expats think they have to purchase something online before they go and that can end up impractical or a bad call. Whatever you pull the trigger and get online might not be the best in your area or doctors might not take it. Some insurance brokers will try up upsell you or sell you insurance to a place they know nothing about. I'd advise waiting until you get there and seeing what's best for you or your family's situation.

Medical Tips Before You Go

- Request extra medication before moving.
- Visit the doctor, dentist, optometrist, and whoever else beforehand.
- Make sure you've got enough glasses and contacts.
- Have copies of your medical records scanned and saved.
- You should know the drug name and dosage of what you're taking not just the brand name.

You can run the same risk of big medical bills abroad that you can in the states if you're not properly insured or don't have the cash. There are databases you can look up of English-speaking doctors around the world and you'll be surprised how multilingual the medical field abroad is. Especially if you're in expat areas it'll be a simple process to locate English speaking medical staff. Some countries will require some form of coverage before granting you more permanent residency, such as European nations.

Insurance Resources

- IAMAT.org - To find English speaking doctors.
- AllianzTravelInsurance.com
- HCI Group
- CignaGlobal

For Nomads Check Out

- World Nomads
- Safetywing.com

Note: I don't recommend any one insurance over another. Everyone has different and unique needs, and your country choice weighs a lot into your healthcare decisions. There are lots of international travel and insurance options to choose from. I don't personally have any health insurance other than the Foreign Medical Program of the VA, when I get sick I go to the pharmacy or just pay for a clinic.

Every veteran is going to be different whether it comes to using Tricare, the Foreign Medical Program, ChampVA, or international healthcare plans. What you can also do abroad is simply pay out of pocket, and you'll be surprised how cheap it is. Last time I got sick, I just went to the pharmacy and paid for some antibiotics and in two days felt fine. It cost me five dollars.

For Military Retirees

You can use your Tricare benefits in virtually every country in the world with a little information and forward planning. All Tricare plans cover emergency care around the world.

- Tricare Locator[25]: Use this link to find an approved Tricare provider in your desired country.
- Tricare on Facebook[26]
- Tricare Facebook Group:[27] This is an unofficial FB group.
- Official Tricare Overseas Website:[28] You'll find specifics here on your costs, claims, etc.
- Tricare Around The World Book[29]

If you are moving abroad on a permanent basis, it makes the most sense to enroll in Tricare Overseas. If you enroll in Tricare Overseas, you'll still have coverage if you travel back to the U.S. It offers multiple plans and you'll have to

---

[25] https://www.tricare-overseas.com/beneficiaries/resources/provider-search

[26] https://www.facebook.com/TRICARE/

[27] https://www.facebook.com/groups/tricareatw/

[28] https://www.tricare-overseas.com/

[29] https://a.co/d/gvhYOUK

decide which option is best for you, Tricare Prime Overseas, Tricare Prime Remote Overseas and Tricare Select Overseas.

In the majority of cases, you'll have to pay out of pocket up front for medical care overseas through Tricare. In some cases, you'll pay a percentage. This might seem extreme, but the cost of healthcare overseas is usually far cheaper – then you get a bill, get a medical report, file it online and boom you get reimbursed. At least in theory that's how it's suppose to go.

Note: Keep in mind Medicare is not available outside the United States or it's territories.

Some places will be able to bill Tricare directly, and some medical centers will want you to pay in cash and not a card for your medical services. It's important to note that medications abroad are often far cheaper than in the U.S. If you're paying $20 for a six-month supply of your meds you might not bother turning it into Tricare. Everywhere is going to be different and every situation unique.

If you're abroad and in need of medical advice, contact the Tricare Nurse Advice Line[30] – This is a 24/7 service with chat, video, and call options. You'll need your DoD benefit number handy when you call.

---

[30] https://www.mhsnurseadviceline.com/home

If I have Tricare, do I need additional coverage if I want to live overseas?

That's up to you. Peace of mind is important and having local insurance can be a very good thing. You'll get better at using Tricare the more you do it. This isn't about medical advice, and everyone has different medical needs. It's something you should investigate and make your own decision.

How do I find an authorized Tricare provider overseas?

Outside the U.S. the term *"authorized"* isn't how it works. Technically you can visit ANY provider who is licensed and meets the standards of the medical community. There's no official list but I tell people to start with who they find through the Tricare website provider search. In the potential scenario no Tricare network provider is near you, you'll want to find a local clinic you like. Then you'll pay the bill and submit your claim for reimbursement. I'd advise getting into expat networks to see what hospital or clinic in your area other veterans are using.

Note: *Tricare in the Philippines has its own set of rules.*

3 Steps to Using Tricare Abroad

- Collect your medical report or hospital report. This lists treatments, diagnosis, tests, and medications. It **MUST** include your name, doctor's name, license

#, and the name, address, and phone of the clinic or hospital.

- Get an itemized receipt printed with clinics matching name and have an address or phone number. It should include some type of *"paid"* stamp or indication that you paid whatever bill.

- Ensure you leave with a credit card or cash receipt of how much was paid and that no payment is remaining. Get this receipt no matter what, even if you think you don't need it or it's a minimal amount.

- Submit ALL of these in order to get properly reimbursed.

Service-Connected Veterans

If you are service connected and NOT retired, then you'll want to understand the Foreign Medical Program (FMP) of the VA. This is only for service-connected veterans traveling or residing abroad. You can enroll in the States before going abroad if you want but it's usually quicker to just do abroad. In the Dominican Republic you can do it in a day. You sometimes need access to your EBenefits account if you're enrolling overseas.

I'm going to explain this in plain language – Through the FMP you can get treatment for any service-connected disability as well as a condition that is associated with and aggravating those conditions. You can get treatment for

115

anything rated, including things rated at zero percent. So, it's important to get everything rated before going abroad.

It's somewhat straightforward, you enroll and take the clinic, hospital, or wherever you're getting treatment your service verification letter and rated disabilities. I've had good experiences with the FMP in the Dominican Republic, but it is a VA program, so it's far from perfect. Hopefully the program becomes more streamlined in the future, more and more Veterans are using it year after year so hopefully it will.

I've talked to a lot of Veterans abroad who have had issues with the FMP, I haven't had any living in the Dominican Republic. This is the only place I've used it, it's a distinctly different program and functions differently than the VA.

In some countries, they'll expect an up-front payment for treatment. I've also heard of some places wanting you to pay 25% up front. Every place is going to be different but what's important is that you can get your service-connected healthcare abroad. It's important to reiterate that it's for service-connected healthcare, not general healthcare. Where I live in the Dominican Republic, we have specialized clinics that only treat Veterans. Most clinics abroad are healthcare clinics that also utilize FMP and don't exclusively treat US Veterans. But there are healthcare clinics in Thailand, Colombia and the Dominican Republic that *exclusively* treat US Veterans.

If you live internationally and have Tricare and FMP, you have to choose which one to use for any given claim. With Tricare you'll have a copayment but will get your money back sooner. Your money can also be direct deposited when you get reimbursed. In FMP, you'll be fully reimbursed, but it will take longer, and FMP will mail a check. It doesn't currently offer direct deposit. You might also have no out of pocket costs with the FMP.

Note: Veterans living in the U.S. who are rated 100% Permanent and Total are eligible for full healthcare through the VA, not just service-connected treatments. This is NOT true with the FMP, which will only cover rated disabilities including those rated at 0%. This is potentially changing in the future, with 100% Vets able to get general healthcare abroad. Keep in mind FMP is a VA program and subject to change.

Dependents of service-connected veterans can potentially receive healthcare through the Civilian Health and Medical Program of the Department of Veteran Affairs (CHAMPVA).

Private Insurance

There's no shortage of private international plans and options. Some veterans want regional coverage in case of traveling and admittedly, purchasing a plan can be confusing. It's going to take a bit of reading and comparison to find the best one for you. But you should have a clear idea of your healthcare needs and acceptable levels of coverage. I don't want to recommend any private insurance because every veteran is going to have a different best option depending on their needs and location.

Travel Insurance

A benefit of travel insurance is often your insurer will work with the hospital to arrange bill payments, and you won't need the cash up front like you do with Tricare. Some Veterans may not have the necessary credit card limits needed for Tricare and on top of that, abroad you never know some places might only take cash or won't accept credit.

Short term travel medical insurance can be affordable and give veterans peace of mind up front until they get set into their Tricare situation overseas. Travel insurance will also usually cover medical evacuation, which can be extremely expensive in emergency situations. It can also be prudent to have travel insurance if you're traveling through multiple countries or nomadic.

Health Care Resources for Travelers From The CDC

The following list of resources may help international travelers identify health care providers and facilities around the world. CDC does not endorse any particular provider or medical insurance company, and accreditation does not ensure a good outcome.

- The nearest US Embassy or Consulate[31] can help travelers locate medical services and notify your friends, family, or employer of an emergency. They are available for emergencies 24 hours a day, 7 days a week, overseas and in Washington, DC (888-407-4747 or 202-501-4444).
- The US Department of State maintains a list of travel medical and evacuation insurance providers[32]. But they do not endorse any one provider or service.
- The International Society of Travel Medicine maintains a directory of health care professionals[33] with expertise in travel medicine in more than 80 countries.
- Travel agencies, hotels, and credit card companies may also provide information on local health care resources.

---

[31] https://www.usembassy.gov/

[32]   https://travel.state.gov/content/travel/en/international-travel/before-you-go/your-health-abroad/Insurance_Coverage_Overseas.html

[33] https://www.istm.org/clinic-directory/

Chapter 13

Taxes, Banking and Need To Know Info

If you think moving abroad means you don't have to pay taxes back home, think again. America is one of two countries in the world with a citizenship-based tax system. Which means unless you're willing to renounce your citizenship, you'll be dealing with the IRS for the rest of your life. I would not renounce my citizenship or advise anyone to do that. Despite the perhaps contradictory theme of this guide, I love America and am intensely patriotic. Renouncing your citizenship is the ONLY way you can end your relationship with the IRS.

"Your worldwide income is subject to U.S. income tax, regardless of where you reside."

~ The IRS

There are things you can claim to help alleviate your tax burden if you're working abroad or for a foreign company such as the Foreign Earned Income Exclusion and Foreign

Tax Credits.[34] I don't want to provide specific tax information because so much is subject to change. I have a master's degree from Harvard but don't fully understand my own taxes. Our system is overly complicated and lots of people and companies take advantage while a lot of other people get screwed over. I usually think I'm on the getting screwed over side.

There are expat focused accountants and H&R Block has an Expat Tax Filing System. There are other tax companies that will understand the ins and outs of expat life. I will let you know that the United States government is the only government in the world that chases and pursues its citizens abroad with persistence to hunt down their money. For example, the guy who ran up across the border from Guatemala is not being sought after by the Guatemalan government to send money back for tax purposes. But you will get hunted down by the IRS so I would make sure to continue to pay all your taxes.

Banking

You need to bank with a strategy, or you're going to end up paying a ton of money in fees, conversion rates, transfers, and ATM charges. Opening a bank account abroad is something you should do IF you plan on being

---

[34]   https://www.irs.gov/individuals/international-taxpayers/choosing-the-foreign-earned-income-exclusion

in the country for long term but is not a necessity. There are probably some countries out there I would not open a bank account in if I didn't have faith in the local government or economic system.

My first banking tip is for you to look into a Charles Schwab debit card which is very popular in the expat community that reimburses foreign transaction fees and reimburses you for any ATM fees. This isn't your only option but it's one of the few specific recommendations I'll make as well as keeping at least one US-based bank account open.

You'll want a credit card with no foreign transaction fees, and I'll get into that a bit later. I transfer money to myself using Remitley in the Dominican Republic to get Dominican Pesos, that's the best way there but every country is going to be a bit different. PayPal for example has a lot of fees with international transfers so I would avoid that.

- <u>NerdWallet: 5 Best Ways to Send Money Internationally 2025</u>[35]

---

[35] https://www.nerdwallet.com/article/banking/best-ways-to-wire-money-internationally

- Forbes: Best Ways To Transfer Money Internationally[36]
- Bankrate: How To Make An International Money Transfer[37]

The financial aspect of getting your money can be bane of expat existence, and there's no perfect solution to this dilemma. MoneyGram even banned me on my first transaction because I downloaded the App and tried to send myself $5,000 which they deemed suspicious. MoneyGram isn't as widespread as Western Union, which is in pretty much every country but Western Union fees are high. If you do that make sure you send it in dollars and not the local currency because Western Union overcharges you like crazy on conversion rates.

The US government makes it complicated for foreign banks to work with you when you're living abroad. Non-US banks have to report your assets to the U.S. Treasury Department if you have a foreign account balance over $10,000. As of now you must also file an FBAR (Foreign Bank and Financial Accounts) report to avoid getting into trouble for money laundering. This isn't your taxes; it's a

---

[36] https://www.forbes.com/advisor/l/best-money-transfer/

[3737] https://www.bankrate.com/banking/international-money-transfer/

different thing and not filing can result in the IRS seizing your cash.

This is one obvious reason it's good to have an accountant who understands some of the ins and outs of expat life. A good strategy is to never let your foreign bank account get above $10,000. If you do, even for one day then legally you have to file an FBAR. If you're running a business abroad this can be difficult or if you're retirement check gets deposited into a foreign account.

Social Security Abroad

You can receive your U.S. Social Security in foreign lands except for North Korea and a few other countries. They do offer a Payments Abroad Screening Tool[38] so you can see if you're payments will continue. You do have the right to receive social security benefits while living in another country. If you're a Veteran, the vast majority of the time your social security benefits won't be affected by moving abroad. You can set up a direct deposit to a foreign bank as well that has a international direct deposit agreement with the United States.

---

[38] https://www.ssa.gov/international/payments_outsideUS.html

Understanding SSDI Abroad

If you want to receive Social Security Disability (SSDI) abroad you have to return to the United States every six months for at least one day as of this writing. SSDI is based on your work credits, so you'd need to qualify based on your own work record. You do have to live in an approved country. The countries you cannot receive SSDI are Cuba, North Korea and others.

You are considered to be INSIDE the United States if you live in Puerto Rico, the Virgin Islands, Guam or other territories. Which means you don't need to return to the United States every six months. Just because you move abroad doesn't mean you can't come up for periodic or normal reviews of your benefits so you might need to return for that. If you meet the usual criteria for SSDI, you can continue to receive it abroad.

Note: *Supplemental Security Income or SSI is different than SSDI, you cannot receive SSI outside of the country.*

Chapter 14

Teaching, Volunteering and Part-Time Work

My first job abroad was teaching in Thailand, and it was amazing. I did a Teaching English to Speakers of Other Languages (TESOL) certification in person in Bangkok where they set you up with a job upon graduation. My TESOL class was eight people from different countries, and I was one of two Americans.

We all became friends during our teacher training, would help one another and adjusted to life in Thailand together. Two of the people are still living there in Thailand years later teaching and loving life. English is the most common second language in the world and a lot of schools want native English speakers to be teaching. Teaching English abroad can be your ticket to seeing the world while working a stable and rewarding job.

I went to school in the states to be a teacher and it was pretty quick in my student teaching experience I thought to myself, *"I can't do this."* I was fresh out of the military and couldn't really believe I was getting cursed at my 8th graders for telling them to take off their headphones. I had a young bully call a lot of mean names to a girl, I kicked him out of class and recommended he be suspended to the assistant principal.

We called the mother, and she came up to the school to meet with us and when I told her what he had said, she replied *"he said he didn't say that."* I explained to her that I had heard him say it, along with probably thirty other people. She told me she had just met me, and she believed her son over me. Honestly, I couldn't believe it sitting there in my shirt and tie that this woman thought I would just make this up for no reason.

My first day teaching in Thailand all the students bowed to me, listened, and were respectful. They treat teachers with an immense about of respect in Asian countries and after being in the military I enjoyed my experience there. The school I taught at only wanted me to teach about four lessons a day, so I would have time to grade papers and prepare. With my teaching salary and my military retirement, I was living a great life in an amazing apartment in Bangkok.

I was going out to nice dinners, working out, and I loved the kids I was teaching. I had more freedom than I would teaching in the states, and we would do assignments about Marvel movies and the kids would act out scenes to practice their English. I'd have the students' doing pushups and jumping jacks and counting off like military exercise in English and they loved it.

127

Volunteering Abroad

Putting a stamp in your passport to volunteer abroad is one of the best things you can do and gives you an opportunity to go about anywhere. It can provide a lifechanging experience and a taste of life in other places. There's a lot of benefits to volunteering abroad, it looks great on a resume, and you can network. But at its core it's about giving back.

You might raise an eyebrow when you learn pretty much all the volunteering abroad programs have some sort of fees attached to them. Paying to volunteer feels weird but there's flights, meals, and expenses that go into it. It might also seem wrong to volunteer abroad when there are lots of problems in America. Abroad you can really make a difference and it can be incredibly rewarding. Veterans aren't only a force for good within our country or when we're in service, we're a force for good and make a difference everywhere we go.

I believe expats do have a responsibility to give back to their new communities, in big or small ways. For me volunteering with a youth boxing program in the Dominican Republic has been rewarding. The kids are great, the parents appreciate it, and boxing is one of life's greatest teachers. It keeps me in shape too trying to keep up and provides me with a lot of gratitude for my own life. As a veteran, you're probably looking for ways to serve and this is a good start. But there are lots of opportunities you'll bump into to make a positive difference when you get outside the USA.

Reputable Volunteering Abroad Opportunities

- WWOOFing[39]

- International Volunteer HQ (IVHQ)[40]

- GoEco[41]

- Involvement Volunteers International (IVI)[42]

- SAVE Volunteering[43]

- LOVE Volunteers

Part Time Work

There are some good reasons to look for part-time work even if you don't necessarily need the income. I've met people who've retired young overseas and end up with

---

[39] https://wwoof.net/

[40] https://www.volunteerhq.org/

[41] https://www.goeco.org/

[42] https://www.facebook.com/volunteering.org.au/

[43] https://volunteering.org.za/

too much time on their hands. We think lounging on the beach with a cold beer everyday sounds like a dream life, but that'll get boring faster than you think.

There's an old British guy who works one of the scuba dive shops I go to and he's a retired multimillionaire who just wants something to do and he loves talking diving. He said the dive shop owners never paid him and he's never asked for any money, he just loves hanging out and helping people in his retirement. I'm friends with other people who work part-time abroad doing things they are passionate about. Our Veteran organization, Veterans in Paradise in the Dominican Republic donates all the money we make from our events and T-shirts back into the community.

Benefits of Part-Time Work

- Extra income
- Social benefits
- Set your own schedule
- Physical activity
- Mental stimulation
- Sense of purpose
- Feeling of community

My friend Freddy owns a little beach bar and restaurant and a few days a week I go there, work on my computer and have lunch. We've been friends for a long time, and we talk about sports. One day he confessed to me he never really makes a profit, most of the months he breaks even because he pays his employees more than any other beach spot and he eats all his food there.

Freddy just likes having a spot to hang out, loves owning a restaurant, and is a people person. He's got repeat customers that come in every year, and he likes making people happy and his restaurant family. Working abroad most of the time for expats isn't about getting rich, for Freddy that period in his life is over and he just wants to be productive.

Starting a Business

A lot of expats abroad start businesses, usually to cater to the expat community. When they see something missing, the opportunity to create it is there. Expats often own expat related businesses, like ethnic restaurants and places that sell unique or imported items. Lots of expats and Vets also work in the tourism industry. Expats like yourself often have more capital to work with so opening a business is a simpler process.

I came pretty close to opening a beach bar in the Dominican Republic because I could rent out a spot on the beach for only $300 a month. I decided against it for a few reasons. I didn't want to deal with people mainly but business rules here are different. There are different labor laws and certain protections for local workers and navigating that minefield was unappealing. I like going to the beach but if I needed to go there every day it would get old. Plus, I know myself and I'd probably drink way too much.

A lot of expats are starting a U.S. business and operate it when living abroad, you can do a business structure like a sole proprietorship or an LLC for liability protection and tax advantages. If you create an LLC, select a business-friendly state like Nevada or a state with no income tax like Florida.

Chapter 15

Questions To Ask Yourself

How Do You Feel About Spending Time Alone?

I was shocked at how much time I was spending alone when I moved to Colombia. I was in Bogota and it's such a big city and it was hard to make friends. I didn't speak much Spanish, and I found myself in kind of a depressing routine. I was eating alone, and I just wasn't used to that, I had always ate with others when I was serving or with my family. It took me a getting over that hump, finally I realized I had to be extra extroverted, and I signed up for Spanish classes, dance classes, gym classes and started doing my work at a co-working space instead of at my small apartment. Eventually I broke free but those first few months I struggled and felt isolated.

- Air Force Veteran Sarah in Colombia

We spend a lot of our time with family, neighbors, friends and coworkers. We have our established social circles, local bars and churches. You're going to be spending lots of time alone, especially at first. Making friends as an adult is more difficult than in elementary school. As Veterans we're used to being surrounded by people in our military days and when you're abroad you find yourself alone a lot more than you might be used to.

What's keeping you where you are?

Our kids are both in high school and we're waiting for them to finish up and head off to college or the military themselves. We desperately want to move abroad and travel but it's best for our family if we wait. We don't want to uproot our kids during their final years of school, and we are both Veterans with our 100%. Our kids are going to get their school paid for and we're going to travel the world for a year. It's been fun planning everything and thinking about it, but we still have two more years to go. We've been saving money and planning and we'll be abroad in 2027! We still don't know where we're going to live, we want to start in Europe and then do SE Asia and travel for a while.

- Navy Vets Barry and Maddy

What kind of expat life appeals to you?

I was tired, I had done twenty years in the Army and had two divorces. I honestly just wanted to sit down on a beach and not have a schedule. I wasn't in a hurry to do anything, and I felt old and exhausted. I was surprised when I got to the Dominican Republic that I felt re-energized like when I was eighteen. I was ready to rock and roll, I was excited for life again and I didn't want to just lay on the beach. I wanted to swim in the ocean, dance in the streets and hike in the jungle. It's like a second chance at life and I've lost weight, made friends and now I have a girlfriend that I love and she's showing me everything about the country.

- Army Vet Myron in the Dominican Republic

How old are you?

I moved abroad at forty-two. I did twenty-two years in the Marines and after getting out I felt weird. I felt somehow old and young at the same time. I joined at eighteen and finished at forty, I worked for two years at the VA and after a while I didn't know why the hell I was still working. I had just been conditioned to work, work, work. When I found out they had a VA Hospital in the Philippines, I wanted to go work there. Then I kind of thought, maybe I'll just move there. I got the retirement Visa, I qualified for it, and I've been in Cebu for a few years, and I'll be here for the foreseeable future. Life is cheap here, I'm essentially a millionaire with my retirement and VA compensation.

- Marine Vet Garret in the Philippines

Certain countries favor younger expats, and some countries love retirees who will come in and spend their money there. If you're on the younger side like I was when I moved abroad, you're probably more willing to take more chances. In Thailand as of now, you can't get a retirement visa until you hit fifty years old. Other countries have no age limit on pension and retirement visas. If you're young and relying on your VA compensation and not a retirement, then you might want to pick cheaper countries.

Will You Be Okay Without Your Support Network?

I work online and have my VA compensation. I realized I didn't have anyone I could call when I first moved abroad. If I had some type of emergency, if I got hurt or robbed or needed a ride to the airport or anything. I was used to having my family around me, my friends, coworkers, my VFW friends and more. I had tons of people to call if I needed something and initially abroad, I had no one. My apartment complex security guard was the one helping me with things in Santo Domingo initially, then I met friends at the Veteran center and through expat groups on Facebook. Facebook was a big help but at times I still miss having my stateside support network.

-Army Vet Julian in the Dominican Republic

In America, Veterans have a support network. You've got veteran organizations, the Veterans Administration, nonprofits and more. Then you have your own personal network of friends, family, churches and community. Abroad you'll have to find or rather build your tribe. We have a group of built-in friends in the military, and we get accustomed to that, life overseas is a different story. Your support network won't be there, you'll have to create one and it's not always easy.

What's your job?

I realized with my 100% VA compensation I didn't need to work. I wasn't living large, but life in Argentina isn't expensive. Initially it felt good not working but I got kind of bored. I could go out for steak and wine, which are great here, but I needed something to do. I started an online consulting business, building webpages and doing freelance work and that supplemented my income. I can choose my clients, work as much or as little as I want and it's a good life. It's harder to work abroad, at least here they're always going to give a job to a local instead of a foreigner. So, working online was really the only path for me.

- Army Vet Nathan in Argentina

Do you have skills that you can take abroad or a passion? Money makes everything easier but a lot of Veterans use their time to volunteer, travel and do what they love. As I mentioned earlier, a little bit of money goes further in places like Argentina. The people I see who get in trouble mentally are people that can't seem to create a solid purpose or routine.

What's Your Family Makeup?

I'm single like a pringle and life is great. I was married when I was a young private and like a lot of Veteran relationships, it didn't turn out so great. I think it's easier to be single abroad. Dating is far better, I think it would be a challenge to take a wife and kids or family abroad but lots of people do it. It also means I can go where I want and do things, dating life abroad is better. I'm kind of over the dating scene in the United States, it's a mess. I plan on being single for a long time but maybe I'll meet a Mexican girl here I want to settle down with.

- Navy Vet Ryan in Mexico

Most Veterans who end up abroad seem to be single. Like Ryan in Mexico, I'm single and that makes life easier, or simpler. I have a Veteran friend who moved his mother down to the Dominican Republic with him and he gets cheaper care for her than in the states. Family is an important consideration, both your immediate family and extended. I miss my mother, but she can visit me here and I go home about once a year or so. You can move abroad with a family, it's doable and there will be details further on.

What do you want out of moving abroad?

I wanted to get the hell out of the United States. I felt out of place and depressed. I was struggling with my mental health and PTSD after the military. I knew something had to change, I wasn't exactly suicidal but at times I felt halfway homicidal. It seemed like everyone was unhappy and people were so obsessed with politics, it's all anyone wanted to talk about. Nobody gave a shit about any of that in the Army, at least I don't remember it being so important. Here in Thailand, it never comes up, I live in Phuket and we're on the other side of the world.

- Army Veteran Marcus in the Thailand

What do you want out of moving abroad? Do you want to find love? Escape the stress of the United States, do you need adventure or peace? Do you want to scuba dive, grow your own food, or volunteer? What do you want living abroad to provide for you that the United States does not?

_____

_____

_____

_____

_____

_____

_____

_____

It's never only one thing that makes Americans consider a life abroad, for all of us it's a combination of factors. It's never just one thing, for me my top concerns were my mental health and adventure. For you, it's something else. Staying or going is a tough call but one thing I want to reiterate is that you can go back. Sometimes it's just time to go home.

Once you join the military, you're in and it might be easier to escape than prison but it's still a process. You aren't signing a contract with your new country; you're just a guest there. Going abroad for you might not be a forever move, you'll know when it's time to go home. A lot of expats go abroad for a year or two and realize they got what they needed out of the experience.

Chapter 16

Forging Your Tribe

Community and friendship are more important abroad than at home. You won't have the same connections, familiarities or even acquaintances abroad. You might not know anyone initially, that's one reason we created Veterans in Paradise to help Veterans make connections in the Dominican Republic. Community goes beyond just having someone to have beers with, friends abroad help and support you with all thing's expat related.

It might sound weird to talk about your friends as *"having utility"* but they are valuable resources as well as someone to hang out with. When I moved to Thailand originally it helped me being part of a teacher program and then teaching because it was an easy way to meet people. If you think about how you've made friends in the past - it's school, work and organizations. But what happens abroad when you've got no school to attend, work to accomplish and don't belong to any organizations?

An easy fix is do all three and add hobbies. Take a language class, volunteer, join a team or attend networking events and hit the gym. Put yourself out there in your new community, I went to a church in the

Dominican Republic near my house. I'm Christian but when I first went, I spoke zero Spanish. I listened to the sermon, did not understand a single word and sat there paying attention and having a good time.

At the end people were really nice to me and some people there spoke English and talked to me and invited me to local activities. Then I made some expat friends at the gym, gyms are always good places for me because I like to work out and I'm comfortable in fitness environments.

There are two categories of friends you'll make abroad, apart from the dating aspect, and those are the locals and your fellow expats. You'll want to aim for relationships within both communities. You should approach making friends in a lighthearted way, nobody likes someone who tries too hard but you should also go about it intentionally.

I was pretty nervous walking into a Dominican church, even though I love Jesus as much as the next fellow but I did it and I'm glad I did. Some older Dominican women were even telling me to come meet their daughters and inviting me over for Sunday meals. I'm glad I went and built connections with the local community; it's helped me a lot to this day.

There's real danger to the loneliness that can accompany Veteran expat life. You have to be good company for yourself and enjoy your periods of solitude. For me, I really enjoy my alone time and that nobody can really bother me abroad. No family members show up, I don't have obligations to go somewhere for someone's birthday and my time is my own. If I'm doing something, it's because I want to.

The most successful Veterans abroad build themselves a team, a squad to surround themselves with for their new journey in their new country. You can't rush making friends or building a community, it takes time so be patient. Be the time of friend you'd want to have and don't be afraid to approach people or strike up conversations.

Before The Move

The internet and social media are going to be your best bet for beginning to build your community abroad. It's easier to move abroad now than ever before, our ancestors used to migrate without even a compass, only the stars and a dream of a better life to guide them. But as anyone with an internet connection knows, more information doesn't necessarily equal more wisdom. The online expat community has its share of morons like the rest of the world. I'm putting out information and resources for fellow Veterans, for friends, for my brothers and sisters.

My friend Sgt Sosua and I created a Veteran organization for Veterans moving to the Dominican Republic. We hold events, put out information and try to build community. We call it Veterans In Paradise and I want to let you know there are other Veteran organizations around the world.

US Military Retirees and Veterans Living

Abroad Facebook Page

The Facebook group above is a great resource, it's spread around the world, and you might be able to find a Veteran or two in your new country. It's a group of Veterans talking about healthcare, retiring abroad and things like Space A flights. Facebook is a great resource for area specific information, if you want to move to Mexico you'll search Mexico Expats and the more specific area you get the better off you'll be. If you want Veterans in Puerto Vallarta, Mexico, then you'll find a expat group there. Even better for Puerto Vallarta you'll find an American Legion with lots of Vets.

Facebook should be your first move, probably before Instagram and TikTok where you might find a few of those idiots I mentioned above. A lot of people on social media will try to sell you things, courses to move abroad, pay for consultations and more. I'm sure there are good resources out there, especially country specific information. But proceed with caution when it comes to that.

Secondly, before you touch down in your new country, I'd click through some expat information online and watch some YouTube videos. I tend to be a little critical of most YouTube stuff, there's great content and information out there but a lot is for clicks. A lot of the YouTube crowd is international realtors.

There are some expat message boards and a lot of the expat community is very supportive and helpful. There are great networks out there and are designed to be good wells of information. They are updated with information, many are out there and it's best to kind of cherry pick information from different sources.

Expat Sites

Internations.org

Expat.com

GoExpat.com

ExpatExchange.com

My Veterans Living Abroad Blog[44]

Veteransinparadise.com

#

---

[44] https://www.johnhdaviswriter.com/category/veterans-living-abroad/

YouTube Channels

Expats Everywhere

The Global Expats

Vagabond Awake

Amelia & JP

Sgt Sosua

My Youtube: Combat Vet Abroad

I got to self-promote a little bit, it's my book after all so make sure you subscribe to my YouTube and follow me on social media and all that. We also have our free newsletter on our website Veteransinparadise.com. You can look up some expat blogs in Spain, Japan, Colombia or wherever you want to go. If a place exists, in today's world there's some content on it and it's up to you to decide whether that content is beneficial.

In the *"Before you move"* stage, be sure to get secondary confirmation of any information. I wouldn't ever fully rely on one source. Even governmental websites can be incorrect, and the reality is lots of information is constantly changing. Every expat has some bias about some things, I'm passionate about the best countries for Veterans but not every Veteran is going to fit in any box. We're all very different people and there are Veterans that don't want to be around other Vets, I get that.

I tell Veterans if they come to the Dominican Republic, I usually tell them the first beers on me and I'm happy to let them know about life there. That one beer sometimes turns into ten but that's how you make friends. One guy I connected with recently booked the wrong hotel, on the wrong side of the island and ended up in a bind when he landed in the Dominican Republic late at night for his first visit. He hit me up on Instagram and he crashed in my spare room and we got him a hotel the next day.

Expat Friends

It makes the most sense initially to form community with your fellow expats, those are the people you have the most in common with. They've been where you've been, they've moved abroad and gone through the ups and downs of a new area. They've left America, or their home country and will have valuable resources for expat life there. They speak English and if you can link up with other Veteran expats, that's the best resource.

They've assimilated, to some degree and have been through some of the same issues. They are kind of a group of pirates on the same ship. They've got interesting backstories and bring different things to the table. Expats tend to be unique and fascinating people because they, like you are individuals who've gone against the grain. They've swam upriver and gone against expectations, they aren't always perfect and some of them are great and some are terrible. The expat crowd is a circus and different in every area. You've got one thing in common with all of them, you're not a local.

Advantages of Expat Friends

- They're going to relate to your experiences.
- They're going to have unique tips on restaurants, prices, and all things assimilation related.
- They'll be on the same type of schedule and routines that you are.
- They are going to be able to plug you into contractors, handymen and all the things that an expat needs.

Disadvantages of Expat Friends

- They tend to leave and there's lots of goodbyes. They are travelers.
- You can easily get trapped in an expat bubble and forget local friends.
- They might be jaded or whiny. Some of these people are awful humans who are running from something or taking the worst of themselves abroad.

My Expat Friends

Anthony came to the Dominican Republic around the same time I did, during Covid. We bonded on being new to the Dominican Republic and being Veterans. Years later we're still friends and thriving in different ways. We hang out weekly and I visit him at work because on top of being a Veteran, he's also international DJ Bad Habits and works in the Dominican Republic.

We both built lives here, we try to get together around the first of every month around our Veteran payday for some day drinking and hanging out. What I love about Anthony is that he's generally good natured, just a good dude and there aren't many like him. We check up on one another, hit up dinner here and there and work to help the Veteran community.

Anthony is one of those guys that just got fed up with the states, tired of the high cost of living and sick of the toxic dating culture and decided to bail. He medically retired from the military and then retired from the VA. He loves music and being a DJ and now is the man at the one of the most popular bars in the Dominican Republic.

Shawn is sort of my role model, he's a good mentor for me and a complete lunatic. The guy only wants to work out, that's pretty much is life. We've trained Muay Thai together in Thailand, wrestled on beaches in the Dominican Republic and he lives life more intense than anyone I've ever met.

Because of him I got into scuba diving, he's been living abroad and traveling a lot longer than me. He likes adventure tourism, going to places like Iraq for fun. When he's in the Dominican Republic we meet up at the gym, get breakfast and talk life. He was a Marine for a few years then did a twenty-year stint policing and now does whatever the hell he wants. He doesn't drink and I drink too much so it's a good balanced friendship.

Shawn is a traveler, that's what he loves and he's one of those friends that will always hold you accountable. There's no slack with Shawn and I love and hate him for it. He's a good friend to call and even though he's always on the move like me, we stay close.

Pat is the coolest, he's a former boxing champion that realized his money goes a hell of a lot further in the Dominican Republic. He's got great stories, and he started a boxing program in the Dominican Republic for kids. I help him out here and there, holding mitts for the kids and buying equipment. He speaks fluent Spanish after moving there and knows a lot about the local community. Pat gives back a lot, helps a lot and gives a lot of kid's chances at a better life.

He also got me into smoking cigars, which might make him a bad influence but we only live once. The Dominican Republic has some of the best cigars in the world and it's a fun occasion to go to a cigar bar and talk. When you move abroad, there's nothing wrong with living life to the fullest. A lot of us aren't sure in the United States how to live our lives to our fullest but now it's your time. Pat taught me a lot about life, relationships and friendships.

I remember moving into a new apartment in the Dominican Republic and immediately Pat brought over a housewarming gift, a bottle of wine and a good cigar. He was my only friend that did that, who made the effort. He's taught me a lot about being a friend, even with his own distractions, struggles, custody battles and more Pat's always been there. It's important to have friends like that abroad, real friends that will be there when you need them.

You always want expat friends you respect. A lot of expats unfortunately take the worst of themselves abroad. Pick expat friends you admire, who better you and who you'll be proud to be around. Who you choose to associate with says a lot about you and some expats will try to take advantage of you. A lot of other expats will lead you down bad paths and even encourage bad investments.

I've hung around the wrong crowd as a teenager and abroad. Because it does feel a little bit like a teenager experience abroad, where you choose to spend your time is going to determine your day to day. A lot of Veterans, usually male Vets link up with guys that sit at bars and drink all day, that isn't the kind of expat life you want.

Local Friends

Building local friends takes time, especially if there's language barriers. One of the best things about speaking English is everyone speaks a little bit. Everyone knows

American movies and culture. People want to practice English if they don't speak it, from taxi drivers to bartenders. Local friends can be more difficult to make but worth the effort if you're going to be somewhere long term. Learning the language goes a long way but wherever you go in the world, people will speak English.

Many Vets get stuck in an expat bubble, that's where they feel comfortable. But everyone in the world knows our culture and now you can learn about theirs. Your new country has pop culture icons, movie stars, musicians and historical figures. Learn about the goings on there, who people respect, history as well as popular and despised figures.

A hundred years ago, what would I have in common with a local person in the Dominican Republic? We wouldn't speak the same language and google translate didn't exist. Where I live, everyone knows who Cardi B is, she's Dominican, everyone knows David Ortiz, he's Dominican, and everyone knows Al Horford because he's a professional athlete. Dominicans all know American culture and the whole world even watches the same shows on Netflix.

Connecting through the local culture, even with our American lens will help you connect with people. Baseball is king where I live, people love baseball from local teams to national stars. I'll go to local games, drink some local beer and cheer on whoever. When I lived in Thailand I would go to the local arenas and watch Muay Thai fights. Everywhere has popular events and you should make it a point to check it out.

Wherever you go in the world, the local people are passionate about something. They want to get fired up and cheer on Friday nights, no matter what it might be. In Brazil it might be Jiu-Jitsu or soccer. Local friends are going to be harder to make than expat friends and they might be a little more guarded. They know you're a foreigner in their land or honestly, they might be thinking what they can get from you.

Being a good person, a good expat goes a long way towards making local friends. It's easy to get jaded in a new environment. The people most eager to meet you are often the last people you want to be friends with. But that doesn't mean everyone's bad or has malicious intentions. People are people, of course they are self-serving. We are humans, we want to be happy, enjoy ourselves and have peace in our lives. Most of my expat friends are all Veterans or retired cops or somehow related to fitness, martial arts or something like scuba diving.

My Local Friends

I met *Alexei* one of my first weeks in the Dominican Republic I attended a local nightclub, as I am prone to do. I met a big bouncer there, who obviously was into fitness and working out. I asked him about local gyms, fitness and had a quick conversation about working out there. He told me that if I wanted, I could go work out with him at a local gym outside the tourist zone that he goes to. So, I went there the next day, met him and we worked out together. He introduced me to other local bouncers and then all the local bouncers at bars and security guys all knew me. People tend to respect you more when you're a Veteran and when you're fit.

Then he and I were hanging out at local spots, he took me to places expats usually don't go to. I didn't have to wait in line at the local nightclub anymore because I knew all the security guys. The gym is a great place to meet people, it's a great equalizer. It doesn't matter that I'm a gringo and Alexei is a Haitian guy, we both are doing the same bench press and trying to improve ourselves. Fitness is a shared passion that spans nationalities, and we can all learn from one another.

William is a guy that would probably be rich as hell in the states. He's what you'd refer to as a jack of all trades handyman and I'm super happy I know him. I had a problem with electricity in my apartment, half of my outlets would work about half the time. It was a weird situation, and you'll find this type of thing abroad. My landlord at the time, we had an unspoken agreement he keeps my rent super low and I don't bother him about the apartment. It was a great apartment and a good deal but not the best when the outlets aren't working correctly or go in and out.

William fixed my electrical problem and informed me of a new problem, my neighbor was stealing my electricity. William's English isn't so great, and he laid it out for me as best he could that my neighbor had hooked his air conditioners up to my meter. Coming from the states I was new to this; he was stealing my electricity? That felt weird, like my oxygen or my water. He showed me the wires and I was so fucking mad. My neighbor at the time was an American dude, named Nick and I'm putting his name in because it's a true story. That was why my electricity bill was always so high.

William helped me, beyond my electricity issues, with just getting into the local community. He had a wife and three kids in my town, and he's been a good friend. Will has looked out for me, been there for me, endorsed me and just generally been supportive. I went to the local river for his birthday celebration, brought some bottles of rum and we had a great time. He's reputable in the community and has helped us out a lot with our charity endeavors.

I met *Johnny* at church. I always make fun of him because he's got seven freaking kids and that to me seems insane. I call him a baseball manager because I assume he's going for nine kids. He's a great human, at least most of the time and a great father. Johnny is a great person to be around.

He helps me negotiate for a lot of things and when I wanted to buy a golf cart, I asked him to look around.

Johnny found me a really good deal and when I showed up the owner, a golf course manager was a little mad some white guy was showing up with cash and not Dominican Johnny. But that's life and we all got over it, now I have a sweet golf cart so I'm not complaining. Johnny can get better prices for me for big purchases, that's the way life goes. I took him out for dinner and drinks, and we called it even for him saving me a bunch of cash.

Dig Into Who The Hell you Are

To build your new tribe it takes knowing the Veteran in the mirror. Your core values, your passions, your vices and your goals. A lot comes to mind when you think about your identity, every veteran is a complex, crazy, and unique person. You start at the surface and then you go deeper from there. We're all different and what I love about moving abroad is that it gives you a chance to dive into who the hell you are. In every aspect, the good and the bad and for the first time you can explore that. You don't have to be who the world tells you that you should be, no way. You can be who you want to be. Like a lot of us, I wasn't really sure who I was without the military. It took time to figure it out.

When it comes to friendships, a lot of the time this means exploring yourself. I was shocked at a guy that I deployed with ended up a weird hippie yoga instructor in Mexico. We deployed together, been in firefights and here he is an entirely different person outside the military. We all go through transformations, and you shouldn't let anything limit your potential. We can be multiple people throughout our lives and whoever you were in your past life in America isn't who you need to be in your Veteran expat life.

My Identity

I utilize my own stories in my writing because that's what I know. Even though you and I might not know each other, we have things in common. We're both Veterans, we have those shared military experiences, lingo and values. We both have courage; we signed on the dotted line and we're willing to die for our country and for our fellow servicemembers. We're both American, we're both interested in travel and we're pursuing a different kind of life after military service. If you're the type of person that would read this book, we'd be friends.

John

American Veteran- That's who I am, that's what defines me and the military was the most shaping experience of my life. There are so many Veterans abroad, I've been shocked that I'm the first person to write about it.

To me, that American Veteran identity is what builds my Veteran expat identity. The veteran friendship goes beyond the casual into the heart and soul. No Veteran has the same experiences, training or story but we all have a few things in common. We are all warriors; explorers and we've been willing to literally die for our country and friends. No sentiment is greater than that, the Bible says, *"greater love hath no man than this, that a man lay down his life for his friends."*

Fitness- You might not know it looking at me, but I love fitness. You might not know it because I also love food and alcohol. Gyms are an awesome place to meet people, both local and expat and people are more authentic. Gyms are often superior to bars for meeting the right types of people. I've always loved martial arts and although pretty terrible at all of them I think Jiujitsu rooms, boxing gyms and more are great places to meet people no matter your skill level. Plus, staying healthy and active is obviously important after the military and fitness people are often incredibly welcoming and friendly from yoga classes to running clubs.

Christian- I started going to a Dominican church, part of my personal identity is my Christian faith. In the Dominican Republic, faith and God are very important in people's day to day lives. It's the only country in the world with a bible on its flag.

My faith was one way to connect with people in my new country. In the Dominican Republic, if you ask someone how they are doing the response most of the time is going to be "Good, thanks to God." Or in Spanish, *Bien, Gracias a Dios.*

There's a bit more to all of us than simple categories. There's more to me than Veteran, fitness and my faith. I also like scuba diving, cigars, golf and art. There are Veterans of Foreign Wars posts in different countries to meet Veterans, there are apps to meet expats, there's social media and there's going to be more people moving abroad in the years to come. Information is always changing; you are always changing but your identity is something for you to explore abroad.

The point is to never forget to tap into who you are, at the core of your soul. Maybe you're someone that loves to try new restaurants, go do that with friends. If you love learning, go learn an instrument or language and if you don't know what the hell you like then start trying new things. Go explore, volunteer, be adventurous, say yes to things and get outside your comfort zone abroad.

There are a million things about you that are beautiful. Explore not only who you are, but who you want to be when you create yourself and your new tribe abroad. You're no longer trapped in other people's perceptions of you. You're free.

You can be kinder, gentler, have more patience and be into different things. Your life, your new life is totally in your hands when you create your new tribe. A lot of us prefer to stick to our high school clique tables, but that isn't you if you're moving abroad. It's the opposite of you, there's not a group to stick to, program to follow or recipe. You can be who you want, with who you want, how you want. You're not in the military anymore, embrace whatever weird shit comes to mind.

Chapter 17

The Veteran Expat Roller Coaster

The Veteran Expat Roller Coaster is like five stages of grief. It's something every Veteran expat has to work through on their first move abroad. There are ups and downs to it and you'll probably question your decisions and feel sick to your stomach. You're on the ride with strangers and there will be moments of elation and terror and hopefully at the end you get some photos to remember the good times.

The roller coast of moving abroad is different for everyone, but it won't be boring. Moving abroad as a Veteran can feel like you're riding a roller coaster in a dark room. There's a lot of anticipation to it, you feel like you're waiting in line when you're waiting to move abroad. At times during the ride, you're going to feel upside down and shook around and you'll need to hold on. Then when you think it's coming to an end, it's only getting started.

I'm using the phrase roller coaster to explain the whirlwind of emotions you'll go through moving abroad because the military is kind of like that too. You never really get your bearing because the call to up and move or deploy can come at any time. You aren't really in control;

161

you're strapped in, and Uncle Sam is in the driver's seat. At times during the military you're bored, scared, mad and sometimes you wonder why the hell you got on this ride to begin with. That's what moving abroad can be like.

How you experience this ride, however, is up to you. You can be the person on the roller coaster with your hands in the air screaming for joy or the person saying *"fuck, fuck, fuck - let me off"* the whole time. Embracing the ride, with all its twists and turns is going to make for a better experience.

Stage 1: Preparation and Back and Forth Phase

It's an exciting feeling thinking about moving abroad, the planning is a fun aspect. Not being sure, the temptation, and thinking about the things holding you back. It's a little overwhelming to consider and you almost don't even want to tell your friends and family. You're fantasizing about life abroad and how it could play out, both the good and the bad.

You start looking more critically at your own environment and you start thinking more and more about your potential new country. You watch YouTube videos in your free time and you're reading stuff like this, your social media algorithm seems like it's trying to convince you to move abroad. You're evaluating purchases and long-term plans you thought you had. Is this really possible? Are you doing this?

Then something happens, maybe like my friend Keith your car gets stolen, and you just say, *"fuck this, it's a sign."* Maybe a relationship ends, and you think to yourself it's the right time for a fresh start. Then when that moment hits you, you start your preparations, you look at yourself in the mirror and you think, *"I'm really doing this."* When the planning starts you run yourself down some internet rabbit holes, you join Facebook groups, and you start looking for reasons to leave and reasons to stay.

My back-and-forth phase was trying to decide if I was really going to go to Thailand for this teacher program. It looked so appealing and the staff I had talked to were super nice and welcoming. I had the money to do it, and they recommended local hotels near the school I was attending. I read testimonials and they told me they could guarantee me a job if I finished the program.

Making the decision to move to another country is a big step but if you were in the military, you aren't someone afraid of taking big steps. You're a Veteran so throwing yourself into the unknown isn't as scary as it might be for other people. You join the military by yourself, and you get out by yourself. You know moving abroad is a challenge, but with the right planning and strategy you can do it. Then you board that plane.

Check out these moving abroad checklists and design your own:

- Expatica: The Ultimate Moving Abroad Checklist[45]
- Forbes: 7 Steps To Take Before Moving Out Of The United States[46]
- Wander Onwards: 13 Step International Moving Checklist[47]

Stage 2: Honeymoon Phase

The first bit in a country feels like a new romance. All the sights and smells are intoxicating, and you overlook any negative aspects. The newness of everything, the food, friends, and routine are amazing. You wake up energized and go about your day like a detective, figuring things out and happy to get lost and explore a bit on the way. Every day is a new adventure, and you wake up motivated and go to bed tired.

---

[45] https://www.expatica.com/global/moving/relocation/the-ultimate-moving-abroad-checklist-103015/

[46] https://www.forbes.com/sites/kathleenpeddicord/2024/10/11/7-steps-to-take-before-you-move-out-of-the-united-states/

[47] https://wanderonwards.co/international-moving-checklist-how-to-move-abroad/

It feels like you're just starting to get to know your new neighborhood and city and it's just getting to know you as well. Your days feel carefree, and you live impulsively, taking on new experiences with an open mind. You drink more than you should and spend a little more then you should and it feels like vacation. When I first got to Thailand, I told myself I would try to take it easy because I was in a teaching program, but I rushed around Bangkok taking in all the craziness of my new city.

I loved exploring the temples and found the art and history indescribably beautiful. I'd walk around until three in the morning like a kid in a candy factory. I would ride the subway and even the bad parts of the city felt appealing, even the grime and red-light districts captivated me. The beer tasted better, the malls were fun to explore, and I had a ton of energy. There were so many night markets with so much to see and I met new people, started learning Muay Thai and tried a new restaurant every single day.

I grew up with cornfields in my backyard in Iowa so wandering into a red-light district and seeing the debauchery was a new world. I loved the blend of the high culture with beautiful rooftop bars and the street food scene. I went on a lot of dates with Thai girls who wanted to learn English and I was happy to take their recommendations on going here or there and exploring. Flights within the country were about $40 one way to go somewhere so I could hop on a plane in Bangkok and go to Chang Mai or Phuket. The initial honeymoon phase of my first living abroad experience in Thailand was awesome. I was fascinated by everything and everyone, but like any honeymoon eventually it comes to an end.

Stage 3: Oh Shit Phase

The Oh Shit phase comes when you realize, *"Wow, I'm living in another country."* It kind of hits you and forces some reflection on how much you've drastically changed your life. To me, the Oh Shit phase was a good thing, for some people it's scary. It's easy to start second guessing their decision and start wondering about going back. Then they even start wondering what their friends and families will think, remembering all the people that second guessed you.

The people you left behind probably can't wait to tell you *"I told you so."* The biggest comparison is when you decide to exit the military, it feels a lot like that. It's a shock and you have to figure out what the hell to do with yourself, you aren't sure if you should have gotten out or stayed in. The military is a security blanket in a lot of ways, you know you're getting paid, and you know your responsibilities.

Getting out of the military loses an enormous part of yourself and your identity. That's kind of what moving abroad is, you lose some of your American identity. I'm sure you've had Oh Shit moments in your life, from joining the military to getting out to having kids or getting divorced. Veteran life is full of Oh Shit moments.

This phase is usually triggered when you finally have a moment to sit down and think about things. Sometimes it's triggered by a bout of expat loneliness. It's kind of common for this feeling to come out of nowhere, or it might be when you miss a certain event in the states. Maybe it's around the holidays and you're missing your family's annual Thanksgiving get together or maybe a loved one's birthday. You might think the pizza in your new place sucks and miss your favorite pizzeria or neighborhood bar.

You could even feel stuck, like you can't go home and that can lead to depression. You've invested in this living abroad adventure, you've taken pictures to show how cool stuff is and you've told people back home that you're happy. The Oh Shit moment can hit you when you feel you're in over your head, your phone dies and you can't communicate with anyone, or you get lost. You'll hit a low point and a frustrating moment and boom.

This Oh Shit moment passes; it can last a bit, and you might find yourself experiencing culture shock. It's a signal from your nervous system and you might even feel physical effects. You might feel sick to your stomach, get a headache or feel depression.

The Oh Shit phase can take many forms, it can also be a good thing. You might think Oh Shit you did it, you're proud of yourself. You had this dream, and you went for it and now you're fucking living it. You're a warrior and you do the things people only dream of and you can't believe this is your life.

You get to do what you want, spend your time how you want and live how you want. I had an Oh Shit moment when I moved to the Dominican Republic at the beginning of Covid and I left the craziness of the states behind. I was having a glass of wine watching the sunset, I felt peace and what was going on in the United States seemed lightyears away. It felt good.

Stage 4: Comparison and Homesickness Phase

The comparison phase is one that all expats go through, and the unhappy expats never make it past. You start looking at everything in contrast to America or even the military. The Veteran expat comparison trap is when it's easy to start thinking in terms of superior and inferior instead of simply different.

Falling into a comparison phase makes us a lot more homesick. We start thinking about how even the simplest of things abroad can be difficult. When you just want things to feel normal and not so alien. Living in a new place makes you feel acutely aware of the differences of your new and old country. It really makes you think of what you took for granted back in America, like in the Dominican Republic when the power goes out. We take for granted the fact that electricity works, and water comes out of the tap 24/7 for the most part except in the rare cases of things like natural disasters. We take for granted we can communicate clearly in our society in person, over the phone and online.

Social media has drastically accelerated comparison culture and it hasn't been healthy for anyone, especially kids and those struggling with mental health. We have this fake, bullshit window into the lives of everyone from celebrities to online influencers. We can see why other people's lives, relationships and travels are perfect and ours suck. We're fat and ugly and they are fit and beautiful. We've all had that with people in the online sphere and it takes maturity to see through the smoke and mirrors.

Comparison is a normal human event and there's no way to turn it off completely, in the military we compare each other all the time. We wear uniforms with our accomplishments on them so we can see exactly what other people have done or didn't do. The military is one of the biggest comparison cultures out there, at times it's like teenage girls constantly judging appearance, awards, badges, deployments and more.

I started an unhealthy pattern in Thailand of comparing myself to other expats, some of my friends had been there a long time and spoke Thai. I couldn't even figure out how to say good morning in Thai. They were navigating the culture, subway system and life with far more ease than me. It didn't seem like they struggled at all to get things done and I couldn't even figure out how to work a printer in a foreign language. There's real comfort in the familiar, that's why people stay stuck in unhealthy situations.

Use the comparison phase to learn instead of judge. Learn from other expats, learn about the culture where you're at and learn about yourself. The truth is that every expat will struggle from comparing things to homesickness. For Veterans, home can be an odd concept because where is home? We have drivers' licenses from one state, grew up in another and file our taxes from somewhere else.

Homesickness comes when we miss our loved ones, routines or feel isolated. When you're in totally unfamiliar surroundings, it's easy to miss America. Homesickness isn't always about missing home, it's often just your mind resisting change. It's very much in Veteran nature to want a secure environment. When you get a bad case of FOMO and see your best friends or family back home on social media, you might feel like hopping on a plane.

Another thing that can cause homesickness is boredom, if you've got too much time on your hands. Moving abroad might put more time on your daily clock, which is good but can also present challenges. Veterans with more time on their hands might find themselves getting into trouble.

I'll miss my buddies back home when I see a group chat text of them all getting together, I'll miss seeing my nephew play sports and I'll miss my favorite events in the states. It passes, homesickness comes and goes, you're human, be human - Don't bottle it up.

Stage 5: Gratitude and Acceptance Phase

There's a sense of achievement once you hit stage five. That realization hits that you are simply living and existing in your new normal. You'll be able to look back at your mistakes and low points and frustrations and laugh. There's a sense of accomplishment, you did it, you uprooted your life and started a brand new one. You've faced things outside your control, you've adapted, and you've conquered. It's a good feeling when you start feeling at home.

By now you've realized moving abroad isn't a fairytale life with nonstop margaritas on a beach. Part of the real adventure of moving abroad is that noting is predictable, you start getting off the American habit of living in the future and the past and you start appreciating the present. A life abroad built on gratitude is going to be a good life, gratitude for your past military experiences and gratitude for your fresh start.

Gratitude in your Veteran expat life is both a state and a trait. You can experience momentary gratitude for things but once it becomes a more long-term feeling you've reached a new level. You should feel grateful for your service while appreciating what it's provided you. The small things under the surface are what you can start being grateful for in your new life abroad. I'm grateful that in the evening that I can walk a few blocks to a nice ice cream stand on a random evening. I can see the sunset over the ocean and every day feels like an adventure. Being grateful in your expat life will help strengthen the bond to both your new community and the United States.

Acceptance is a little different than gratitude. When you accept things in your new environment, you acknowledge the very real realities of life. It's coming to terms with your new life abroad, including the negative aspects of it. You accept the fact you aren't in America anymore and sometimes things won't make sense. Acceptance isn't giving up; it just releases the need to feel negative emotions about something.

I have to accept that I lose money on money transfers abroad; it sucks and it's annoying but that's life in other countries. I can work on the best deal, research and minimize the loss but there's no way around it sometimes. For me, accepting negative things abroad leads to more gratitude. If I'm annoyed waiting for someone, it gives me time to myself, time to read or write or time to reflect. I'm grateful for that.

Ask yourself what will you be grateful for in your life abroad? Access to higher quality and better food? Getting away from the stress of the rat race? Are you grateful to be living by the ocean or to find a new girlfriend? There's lots to be grateful for in a new environment, hold onto that gratitude for your past, your present and your new opportunities abroad.

I have to accept that the power goes out occasionally in the Dominican Republic. If I don't, I'll increase my stress and anxiety levels for no good reason. When I lead with acceptance, I increase my resilience and resilience is something Veteran expats need. We needed a heavy dose of resilience to survive our military experiences, and you'll need it overseas as well.

When you focus on the good things abroad and accept the things you cannot change, you'll be healthier, happier and more at peace. We might prefer to live in a fantasy world but unfortunately there's no such thing as Heaven on earth.

Tickets Please

Veterans can be weird people; a lot of times we pay far more attention to our headwinds opposed to our tail winds. Meaning we pay attention a lot more to the things working against us than the things we have working for us, we're more likely to lean towards dark humor, negativity and embracing the suck.

We also tend to be extremely hard on ourselves, more so than necessary. Taking that attitude abroad is going to have bad results, because things aren't going to go perfect. There's going to be ups and downs and even nausea and fear on the Veteran expat roller coaster. In the military we learn mistakes can equal life and death but we're not in that context anymore and we're going to do stupid things abroad. We're going to waste money, maybe get ripped off here and there, get lost and make cultural mistakes.

One thing I want you to do when you feel like you've rode this roller coaster, is celebrate. Celebrate the fact that you feel at home, at least somewhat in your new environment. You've transitioned to a new life abroad like it's your new duty station, it wasn't perfect, but you did it. You've got yourself a place to live, you have a routine, you might even have some friends and now you're living your new normal. Celebrating is gratitude because we're acknowledging that something went well, and we aren't taking it for granted.

If you don't fit this pattern, don't worry, not everyone is going to. It's all part of the process and second guessing yourself is normal. Moving abroad has a lot of ups and downs. One of my frustrations with the expat community is that to a lot of them, it's a weird competition. If I say I pay $800 for rent, they pay $600 for a nicer place. If I traveled here, they've already been, it's a community of one upper individuals.

It's annoying and they all act like they have life all figured out, they know everything, blah blah blah. But I'm telling you, Veteran to Veteran it's perfectly okay to struggle abroad and to go through challenges. Coming through and conquering your low points give you the most growth. So, learn from the expat community, message boards, Facebook groups and YouTube videos…but take it all with a grain of salt.

At the end of the day, in my opinion the Veteran expat roller coaster is worth riding. It's worth even getting sick to your stomach for the adventure and rush of it. You'll grow for the experience and life will never be the same. In a way, the ride doesn't end, and you might cycle again through the phases. As long as you stay on the ride, I promise it'll be an adventure. That's why we joined the military, for the adventure and moving abroad keeps that adventure rolling.

Chapter 18

10 Tips For Veterans Moving Abroad

1. Visit Before You Move

It's hard to imagine something more important than visiting and checking things out before you pull the trigger. It might not be an absolute necessity but it's certainly smart to get your eyes on things before you change your entire life. It's a little costly to take what's essentially a scouting trip before your real move but it's necessary. Moving somewhere with never visiting is on the expat no-no list. Unless you've got significant experience in your desired country, don't move without doing a recon.

Vacationing somewhere is a lot different than moving, a lot of people want to live where they vacation but that isn't a long-term lifestyle. You can't live every day like you're at an all-inclusive resort. What feels right for a week or two might not be a good permanent move.

2. Finding a Place To Live

A lot of Veterans think they need a place to live before they go abroad. I've found this to occasionally be a bad strategy and lead Veterans into bad living situations. It's usually a surefire way to spend more money. It's almost a guarantee that anything you find on the internet is going to have an inflated price. It's harder to negotiate over the phone or through e-mail and renting somewhere sight unseen is a bad policy.

If you're looking to rent, there's literally always apartments for rent everywhere. There's no such thing as needing to put money down now or get it immediately because rentals in expat areas are easy to come by. A lot of the best rentals won't be listed online, because the best stuff doesn't make it that far and a lot of locals don't know how to post online in English. A lot of the best apartments are filled with connections and word of mouth.

As a serial expat, I've found some decent strategies for finding apartments. Nothing will ever replace being on the ground and hunting yourself. It's your place and the onus is on you. It's always good to connect with the local expat community, especially Veterans. How you go about finding a place depends a lot on where you're wanting to go. It's actually easier to find a place abroad than it is in the states, it's a different real estate world.

One of the keys is to have cash, if you've got cash in your hand then you can find a place to live. When I found my first long-term apartment in the Dominican Republic, I paid for a year up front and got a free month out of it.

Those types of deals or even living in hotels and things like that are more common overseas.

It sounds kind of weird to say based on American rentals but go to an area you want to live and walk around. People in most parts of the world still just put signs in windows or outside apartments and houses that say Apartment For Rent with a phone number. There are great options online as well, but the farther you get off the grid the more you need to look offline. My apartment is in a great area and when I walk around my neighborhood, nothing nearby is listed online but there are a few signs to rent and buy.

Don't be afraid to rent a hotel or Airbnb for a week and then find your apartment. That's usually the best way to go about it. Have yourself a good time looking for a place and talking to people and asking for recommendations. You can set up some appointments to look for places before you get down there. Keep in mind when you're looking for a place where a lot of rentals are commissioned based, so whoever helps you get an apartment will probably get a cut. In most areas abroad, especially where there are lots of expats, long-term furnished rentals are easy to come by.

3. Google Drive

Scan and put all of your important documents online so you have access to them wherever you go. This is everything from your DD214 to your social security card to photos you want to save. I always make sure to store all my tax records, leases and any documents into my Google Drive because I'm pretty good at losing paperwork. Other options to do this include DropBox or OneDrive. Google Drive is the best for me and free with lots of storage space.

You don't need to take copies of paperwork everywhere but having access on your phone and on your computer is helpful. You'll also want copies of your license, passport, VA letters and any family information readily accessible. Putting all your important paperwork in an online database just makes sense and streamlines your life. You don't want to need a copy of your DD214 or passport or tax document and not be able to access it abroad. I think Google Drive is your best option but do what works for you.

4. Your Passport

Your passport is now your most sensitive item. There's nothing more important for a Veteran expat. Before you go abroad, you'll want to have it renewed and have enough blank space. Even if you've got a few years left, go ahead and renew it for peace of mind and get the extended booklet for more pages. Some countries will take up a whole page of your passport book with visa information and some will just stamp you or occasionally not stamp you at all.

You also want a copy of your passport, not only in your Google Drive but also a few hard copies of it. You might need a paper copy of your passport for an apartment rental, big purchases or other random things abroad. I always have two copies of my passport with me in my suitcase, in case I need one for an apartment or car rental or something.

Every time I go somewhere, I have a few copies of my passport in my suitcase, a photo of it on my phone and a copy stored online. Losing your passport abroad is a huge pain in the ass and you feel like an idiot going to the embassy. If you lose it and you don't even know the numbers on it, it's more of a suckfest.

A lot of countries will require you to have six months left on your passport before granting you entry, I don't know why it's just how it is. If you expect to take a trip with a few months left, you could be denied entry. Your passport is your identity, more so than your license abroad and you'll need it for consular access, healthcare, employment opportunities and everything else overseas.

5. Travel Insurance

The United States of America official State Department recommends Americans traveling abroad have travel insurance. You can get travel insurance, travel medical insurance or both. Travel insurance pays for things like canceled trips, lost bags, car rental coverage and delays.

There are different levels of it and then there's increased coverage levels with medical insurance.

Travel medical insurance is going to cover the unexpected health emergencies you could encounter abroad. This is everything from getting food poisoning to a serious accident skiing. It'll cover, or is supposed to cover things like ambulance services, x-rays and necessary prescription drugs. It won't cover routine care or things that they don't deem to be *"medically necessary."*

One thing travel insurance won't cover is medical care when you get back home because of something that happened on your trip. So, if you go abroad, break your ankle then get it checked out when you get home, it usually won't cover that. It also usually excludes most mental health care and any problems or injuries you sustained if you're drunk or high or suicidal. If you hurt yourself while drunk or high, at least pretend to be sober when you go to the doctor.

Peace of mind is a valuable thing when it comes to your healthcare while living and traveling abroad. A routine trip to a clinic when you fall ill overseas is generally going to be far cheaper than in the United States. There are many good healthcare options out there, many of them are going to be better in certain places or more suited to your needs than others. You might want it all, so you have confidence abroad and pay extra for things like evacuation insurance. Or you may want only minor things covered.

Most expat blogs and resources will recommend you get some sort of travel insurance before going anywhere. But as I said in the beginning, I'm not a health expert and I'm not telling you what to do or how to spend your money. We all know insurance companies work to not pay out and often come in under reimbursing you. I've had travel insurance in the past when I was bouncing around different countries but don't have any now. I never needed to use it so stopped renewing it and when I tried to use it for something small, it didn't cover what I needed.

6. Pets

Most locations have similar requirements when it comes to taking your pet with you on your new adventure. I know you can't leave them behind and that's a lot of people's first concerns when it comes to moving abroad. I know a few Vets I've talked to that are just kind of waiting for the dog to die before buying the one-way ticket overseas.

Every location is going to require a letter of health from a veterinarian, and it is supposed to be from a USDA accredited veterinarian. This paperwork will need to be within a certain timeframe of your travel. Obviously, a letter from a veterinarian a year prior saying your animal is healthy enough to fly isn't going to cut it.

Your dog or cat will need to be up to date on all vaccinations and might have to have a more current rabies shot for some countries and airlines. Remember that countries can have different requirements than airlines, some airlines might allow certain sizes and breeds to follow but some countries might not allow certain breeds like pit bulls. People stress more about their animals flying I think than their kids most of the time but it's a pretty easy process. You're not the first person to fly with a dog. My roommate has a dog that he brought from the United States to the Dominican Republic, it's not difficult it's just some extra money and paperwork. He was surprised when he got here and Dominican authorities did not care at all about his paperwork that he paid a bunch of money for.

For Veterans with service dogs, it's important to understand that the *Americans with Disabilities Act*, the ADA is only in America and other countries don't have the same protections of service animals. In America you can pretty much take a service dog with you anywhere and everywhere, abroad is different. I've never seen a PTSD type service dog in the Dominican Republic, it doesn't really translate across cultures. So don't expect people to just automatically understand in other countries the concept of a service dog for PTSD or an emotional support animal.

You'll need to meet the same requirements when you leave the country as well or if you're traveling to a new one. This could include more translation of documents for the pet or different requirements for another country. To bring your dog or cat back to the states, you'll need to find an accredited veterinarian again and go through the same process.

7. Driving Abroad

In Mexico and Canada your United States license is good to go. A lot of places will honor your license from the states, and you'll be good to go to rent a car or scooter with your license or just your passport. Don't give your actual passport to anyone when you rent a vehicle, just a copy or a photo. Again, never give your actual passport to anyone unless it's only to make a quick copy. If you do, you can be assured they will be scamming you when you get back and refusing to give your passport back.

Countries greatly differ in their licensing and you're also probably aware in a lot of places they drive on the other side of the freaking road. I'm so American that it's too hard for me to get used to. You can go to Internationaldrivingpermit.org and this will give you a license in over 100 countries. It'll be good for some countries but if you were to hand it to certain police officers, they would have no idea what it is.

It's important to remember this is not a substitute for your actual American license, you're still supposed to carry that too. In the United States, you'll want to get your IDP (International Driving Permit) through AAA. It's very cheap and easy to obtain and can provide peace of mind driving abroad. There are also scams online that offer fake international drivers licenses, make sure you get it through AAA.

In most developed nations you'll just need to have your license, get a visa, take a test and pay some cash to get a license there. Some places, like the Dominican Republic where I live there's no need to really get a local license. Check the requirements of where you're going or traveling beforehand if you're interested in driving. Most places you can rent a car with an American license and passport copy, plus a credit card obviously. Everywhere is going to be different as every country has different regulations regarding operating motor vehicles, motorcycles and boating.

8. Make Friends Online

All the rules we learned to live by as kids when it comes to stranger danger we throw out in the modern world. Especially when you're a Veteran expat. Put yourself out there on the internet, it feels weird for Veterans, but you need to do it. Post in Facebook groups, search and ask your questions and go to meet ups. Ask people to tag along, join games, classes and whatever else is going on in your community to meet people.

Expats and the online community really go hand in hand, utilizing social media to meet likeminded people is important. I've met a lot of friends through gym stuff, language classes, scuba diving and Veteran events that I've discovered online. There's everything from dating apps, Facebook groups, expat platforms to Instagram and TikTok. To meet friends abroad, you have to be intentional, you have to take your internet connections to the real world. There will be linkups for expats in your area as well as restaurants, gyms and other places that are frequented by expats. Especially locations like coworking spots, expensive coffee shops and expat owned and operated bars.

Linking Up With Other Expats

- Internations
- Meetup.com
- Couchsurfing
- Bumble BFF
- Girls Gone International

9. Some Things Are Cheaper, Some Aren't

Inexperienced travelers move to a new place and assume everything is going to be cheaper. That isn't really the case and in fact some things can be more expensive abroad. If you move from New York City to Medellin, Colombia - you'll see that it's like 70% cheaper. But that doesn't mean everything is going to be 70% cheaper across the board.

In the Dominican Republic, electronics like iPhones and flatscreen TVs are more expensive than in the United States. In the United States, avocados can be pricey, well I have avocado trees in my backyard and can pick them for free. I'm eating local chicken and rice or fried fish, obviously it's very affordable. I'm American and a cowboy, so I drink bourbon. That's more expensive here. Good cigars, however, are very cheap. Or I could stop drinking and smoking and save all that money I guess but let's be realistic. Rent is obviously cheaper, transportation is cheaper, and going to the beach is free.

International taxes, tariffs and import fees can impact pricing. If you're looking to buy something expensive, like certain electronics, then it can be better to buy before you go abroad opposed to there. A lot of things impact pricing, including things like shortages and corruption so keep that in mind when buying overseas.

10. Trust Yourself

You're a Veteran, you've got at least halfway decent instincts. When something feels wrong or off, it probably is. Trust yourself in dealing with people, there are lot of locals that will want to take advantage of you. When we think about trust as Veterans, usually we think about our trust in others or their trust in us. But an important aspect of moving abroad is that you need to trust yourself.

When you don't trust yourself, you'll second guess everything. You're going to have to embrace the unknown, it's best to do it with a measure of confidence. You can seek support along the way and adjust fire. You'll make mistakes and learn.

The more research you do, the more you'll trust yourself. You know that preparation equals victory. Every Veteran makes mistakes moving abroad, you won't be the one that does it flawlessly and you'll learn from each one. Trusting yourself is going to go a long way.

Chapter 19

Trial Run

Your trial run is your reconnaissance mission. If there's anywhere, I see people go wrong when they move abroad it's not executing a proper trial run of your area. Living abroad is different, there are unique challenges, isolation and culture shock. Your trial run is an extended period of time visiting a place before making the move permanent. It's not a vacation, it's a mission. On this mission you're looking for reasons not to move there.

During your trial run you're exploring the Veteran expat life, not the tourist life. So many people visit places and think *"I'd love to live here."* But living in Mexico is a hell of a lot different than visiting an all-inclusive resort for a week.

Before You Go

Connect with other expats there before you go, preferably Veterans. Facebook groups are your best starting point. Every area will have a group of expats. Reach into your personal network to see if you know someone who moved abroad to that country or someone from there. Maybe a friend of a friend or someone on a professional network like LinkedIn.

The internet and social media are great resources for this, there's going to be YouTube videos, blogs and more from people living there. One thing that's important to mention about Facebook groups is to remember that it's the internet, so people will complain and whine and bitch. Don't ever fully trust one resource or individual because things change over time.

There are usually get togethers as well in expat areas with these groups and events. I host Veteran networking events in the Dominican Republic and encourage Veterans to come meet other Veterans and find local resources. If you're moving somewhere that has an American Legion or Veterans of Foreign Wars, look into it and attend a meeting. Meet some friends on your trial run and stay in contact.

While You're There

- Walk when you can, that's how you get to know a place. Use public transportation, don't just stick to taxis and Ubers. You learn the most by putting boots on ground and getting a real feel for the place. Take side streets, explore, pop into a local bar and meet people.

- Don't act like you're on YOLO vacation mode, try to live like you would normally. Go to grocery stores, run errands and connect with the local culture as much as you can.

- Explore the surrounding areas, neighborhoods and cities.

While you're there you also want to conduct your *"expat interviews."* This is you talking to other expats about their life abroad, tips and advice. You'll want to ask them a few key questions such as.

- *What don't you like about living here?*
- *What mistakes did you make moving here?*
- *What should I know as a new expat to the area?*
- *Do you have any financial advice for me here?*

While you're there, try to attend a local event as well as an expat event. This can be a church event, local sporting game or fair. You'll want to live in both worlds, the expat world and the local environment. There's crossover between the two but you don't want to only be in your expat bubble. There are lots of ways to get into the local community, volunteering is also a good starting point. You want to be part of your new community, not an outsider to it.

Chapter 20

Apps, Apps and Apps

————————◈————————

When people moved across the country or world in generations past, they lacked that magic little computer we all carry in our pockets. Somehow it makes the world bigger and smaller at the same time and instantaneously connects and disconnects us. One of the beautiful things about technology is that it can make moving abroad easier if you use the tried-and-true apps for travelers and expats.

From learning a new language to understanding currencies to meeting new friends, apps are the golden ticket. Using these apps will help you navigate your new life and make your transition abroad and day to day life a lot simpler.

Wise/Remitley/Revolut/XE Money Transfer Apps

Getting your money as cheaply as possible can be the bane of expat existence. International ATM fees can be high, the conversion rates never cut in your favor, and you lose money getting to your money. There are no perfect ways to do it, but there's certainly worse ways. International bank transfers can often be high, Western Union is everywhere and reputable but a very expensive option compared to others.

I use Remitley in the Dominican Republic to send myself either dollars or pesos, that's the best option here. Talk to other intelligent expats where you're at about the best way to access your money there. Xe is a good app for a lot of places as well and you can send to over 100 countries to get physical cash and transfers. There's not one universal best option, it can depend how much money you're sending, where and the conversion rate they give you. If you're in Asia it's going to be different than in South America.

Whatsapp

Whatsapp is how people talk abroad. In the states everyone texts but pretty much everywhere internationally people use communication apps. Other popular apps are Line and Telegram, many people even communicate frequently through FB messenger. You'll want all three of those apps on your phone in order to communicate with people and businesses abroad.

Taxi Apps

Everyone knows Uber and Lyft but they aren't everywhere and there can be legalities that prevent them from operating in certain places. You might land somewhere and discover Uber has been banned in that country. Other locations have different apps that are frequently used instead but function similarly. In Europe they use FREE NOW, Taxi EU and others. In Thailand they use Grab and Bolt. In India they use Ola, Gojek is in Singapore, Vietnam, Indonesia and the Philippines. BlaBlaCar has a ladies only feature. Careem is used a lot in the Middle East, depending on where you decide to live getting around is a key component and you'll want to use these apps.

Google Translate

Google Translate will be your best friend. There are others but that's the one I primarily use. DeepL is a solid one as well, that's better if you need to translate multiple pages of information or documents. I'm sure in the future more apps are going to get better using AI and soon we'll all have chips in our heads or something. Google Translate is easy, free and can be a lifesaver.

CityMapper

This is a great and underused app and probably the best international city map. They have a lot of supported cities, most places in the world that you would want to go at least. It's great getting from Point A to Point B and will give you prices on things like subways. It'll alert you if you're on a public bus and will say like *"Get off on the next stop"* so it's easy to use. As another option CityMaps2GO is great for offline maps that you can download in case you lose the internet don't have a Wi-Fi connection.

Internations

Internations is great for connecting expats, travelers and global citizens. It has a lot of different area events, with a broad range of things and activities. I don't usually think paying for membership is a good idea unless you're doing a lot of events. The free part of it functions okay but it's your money so it's your decision. Some places it's better and has a lot of events and goings on and some places it's almost nonexistent.

I've also heard there are some scams on there, but you know, it's the internet and expats can make convenient targets. It's a good-looking app and they'll have meet ups, art events and shows. But I'll reiterate that I probably wouldn't pay for the membership, I have a friend who did, and he said it was extremely complicated to get it canceled.

ATM Fee Saver

This app will guide you to free and low-cost ATMs and will tell you the withdrawal fees. It'll also provide important information like what the limits are, such as in the Dominican Republic some banks only let you take out like 12,000 Pesos and other ones let you take out up to

195

20,000. It can also help you locate ATMs and will provide additional information about currency exchanges.

Duolingo/Babbel

These are the best two apps for languages that I've used. You can do them whenever, it's cost effective and you set your pace. I prefer Babbel on my computer when it came to learning Spanish, I don't like the cell phone because it feels like a game or something to me. I paid for it and it's like $75 dollars for six months when I signed up. Then doing it fifteen minutes a day, one lesson per day helped me out a lot.

If you're planning on moving abroad, these are a must to pick up some important language skills. With these apps you can learn anytime, anywhere and target what you want to learn.

Meet Up

Meet Up is a platform where you can organize and find events in your area. They also do a lot of online stuff and it can be good to connect with people before you move abroad. There are a lot of interests and passions in them, like volunteering or hiking groups. A lot of the people are older expats looking to make friends or form community, it felt a little glitchy at times to me but there's definitely good stuff in certain areas. From running groups to church events to wine tastings, it's worth looking into and exploring.

Spotted by Locals

If you're looking to explore an area like a local would, this is a great app to have. The content is frequently updated, and it has some cities much better covered than others. So, if you use it in one city and it's not great, it might be of higher value elsewhere. It provides real recommendations by locals on the best spots to visit, shop, eat and be entertained. If you're looking to get off the beaten tourist path, this is a good way to do it. It also has offline maps which can come in handy, it's an amazing way to find hidden gems that are off the beaten tourist path.

Hostel World

This was my go-to app when I was backpacking SE Asia for cheap stays. Hostels can be a great option to meet people if you're traveling through a certain area or need a cheap stay. I didn't mind this option when I was younger, now I'd probably go with a private room at the hostel but what I love about this app is they have comprehensive and current reviews. These hostels usually have events, free tours and are a great place to meet people in a new city. There are lots of great hostel chains and you can book and stay with confidence, the customer service has also been good for me.

Get A VPN

You'll usually want some type of VPN abroad where internet protection can be less secure. This will give you more privacy and security abroad and reduce the risk of hacking or issues. This is especially helpful when utilizing public Wi-Fi at coffee shops or restaurants. It's also useful for me for my online investments, trading and financial operations abroad. Then I can use a VPN from the states and still watch the shows I want to watch, some of which are inaccessible abroad like HBO. If you work online, you should have a VPN most of the time.

AI Info

There are more AI travel tools popping up and I figure if I do the next edition of this project there will be more. There are pros and cons to AI travel information, it can be compiled and be inaccurate because people post inaccurate information all the time on the internet. It can produce ideas and itineraries that are going to serve more as outlines than complex and detailed plans. You have to be very specific when it comes to entering information and even then, you'll want to verify. Mindtrip is a solid one now and I'm sure they'll have more in the future.

If there's any other apps you know if that are useful for Veteran expats, let me know and if I make a new edition I'll add them. Apps can be a useful tool and can make life easier for someone traveling or living abroad. A lot of people don't think about how similar apps work across different countries. Some apps, like Google Translate are a must everywhere.

Technology is humanity's best friend and worst enemy. One thing moving abroad has kind of let me do, is distance myself from being overly connected. I'll try to do things like leave my phone at home and go to the beach and just try to be more in the moment. Apps and technology are a huge help in moving and living abroad but moving abroad is about living life in the real world. Use technology and don't let it use you.

Chapter 21

Picking Your Country

The decision of where you're going to call home is a tough one and a lot of your life will depend on where you go. It's going to have a huge impact on your experiences and some countries are heaven to some and hell to others. Your life is going to be far different in South Africa than it would be in Belgium. Some places are great for visiting and not so great for living. Some places are terrible for visiting and great for living. Who you are and what you want out of moving abroad is going to be unique for every Veteran.

Sometimes people pick the wrong country and end up with the wrong kind of life. Some people can't handle certain places or environments. I've met Veterans who can't handle the temptations you face being abroad. I've met people who fall in love with a place during a vacation then end up moving there to hate it. Some people just fall in love with the idea of a place, they watch some YouTube videos, and it clicks.

Picking your country is an intensely personal decision, it's like picking a wife or a husband. I've certainly made some bad decisions in the relationship department, but I've been happy and satisfied living in the Dominican Republic.

The Three Perspectives to Consider

The first, always will be the financial perspective. We all might want to live on gorgeous villas overlooking Greek islands, but most Veterans aren't going to be able to afford that. You don't want to go somewhere you can't afford but that isn't going to narrow down your list as much as you might think. Because everywhere is pretty much cheaper than your life in America.

The second is the legal perspective because some places you might want to be, but the visa process is complicated. I love Thailand but they have a more complex system if you want to stay long-term. If you're over fifty there then it's easy to get a retirement visa but I'm about a decade away from that. Some countries you'll need a certain income or to deposit a certain amount of money or you might not want to do visa runs. Some countries want expats there and make it an easy process and others are more complicated. These laws are also constantly changing.

The third is the home perspective. Some places feel right, and some places won't. It's hard to explain but when I came to the Dominican Republic it felt like home. Even after living in Thailand and traveling a lot, there was something about this place that captured my soul. I felt at peace and nowhere else really felt as much like home, even duty stations. For us Veterans, home can mean a lot of things and when you know, you know.

John's Quick Thoughts

> ➤ *A place is like a restaurant. There might be a lot of reviews, and you shouldn't ever 100% believe one person's opinion.*
> ➤ *There are no perfect countries, cities or places.*
> ➤ *Tourism isn't reality.*
> ➤ *Determining why you want to live abroad can help you narrow down your options.*
> ➤ *Let your budget eliminate countries and cities that won't work.*

#

Your Three Choices

You have to come to a decision on your country, city, and your neighborhood. These don't necessarily have to go in order and sometimes you can zero in on the city if you know what you're looking for. Different cities within countries can vary as drastically as they can in the United States. Obviously, life in New York City is a lot different than East Texas. When thinking about where you might want to go, it's best to first evaluate your must-haves.

My Must-haves

- Beach
- Good gym
- Walkability
- Low cost of living

With these things I've eliminated a lot of the world, because a place like South Beach in Miami might meet the first three but the sky-high cost of living eliminates it from contention. Places without a beach can get crossed off too. Then I want to be able to walk or at least take cheap and easy public transportation so that's going to remove a lot of places as well. Everyone is going to have different must haves for their ideal lifestyle. You know yourself better than anyone, there's always pros and cons to everywhere.

Examples of your potential must-haves

- Good schools
- Distance from USA
- Dog friendly
- Safety
- Internet reliability
- Job prospects
- Healthcare
- Marijuana laws
- Weather
- Potable Water
- English speaking
- Pet friendly

- Pollution
- Safe for female travelers
- Ease of property ownership
- Visa rules
- Veteran community

Then there's even more to think about when it comes to immigration laws. Because maybe you found the perfect spot, but you get your visa denied or can't stay long-term. The legal aspect is one thing we all run into during our expat lives. You might find yourself in something of a visa limbo waiting to hear back if your paperwork is approved.

Beyond that there's your hobbies and passions, if you're into hiking then I'm sure you want to be somewhere well suited for that. If you want to sit on a beach all year or surf, then you're going to want to narrow your list. If you love scuba diving, then Roatan in Honduras might be your spot and if you're an avid snowboarder St. Anton in Austria might be your target. What I love about the Dominican Republic is the sun shines pretty much every day, I can scuba dive, swim in the ocean and play golf year-round.

You might have a few must-haves and then you get into your wants. There's always going to be a few tradeoffs when it comes to living abroad. There's no such thing as heaven on earth but there are places that feel a lot closer to it than others.

Country

I've seen Americans shocked to get their visas denied or when they understand the difficult requirements other countries have. The United States is set up to take in lots of immigrants and that's reflected by our culture, when you go other places like Japan for example you see 97% Japanese people. Every nation in the world has an immigration policy and some offer a more streamlined process and in some countries the process is far more difficult.

The most difficult country in the world to become a citizen?
Vatican city.

Your bloodline, where your parents or grandparents are from in some places can help you gain citizenship. This is usually referred to as citizenship by ancestry or citizenship by descent. Americans who have a Filipino parent can become citizens of the Philippines no matter where they were born. That isn't to say you should head back to your family's homeland, but it's something to take into consideration. Lots of Americans are choosing to get second passports based on their bloodline. If you have the race card, go ahead and play it.

A few of the nations that offer citizenship by ancestry

- Ireland
- Ghana
- India

- Hungary
- Italy
- South Africa
- Israel
- Portugal
- Taiwan
- Kuwait
- Australia

Picking your neighborhood

Deciding where to live is one of the most exciting and stressful things for expats. You might have found your city, but what neighborhood and section? This is first impacted by your income and followed by your interests. When I head to a new location, I'll research expat blogs and look up where foreigners are tending to live. These are first usually safe areas and are going to have the things I'm looking for.

The first thing I'm looking for is a good gym. A gym is going to be the only place I'll be going to every day and that's where I'm going to meet people. Once I find a solid gym, either virtually or in person, I find out where the nightlife and restaurants are. Because every day I'm going to work out and every day I'm going to eat. Then I pull up Google Maps and put a pin in the exact location between these two places, so if they are 1,000 meters apart, I'll put a pin at the 500m point. Then I'll go to this exact point, and stand in the street and do a 360, turning around to see what it looks like. If there's an apartment complex here or a sign for rent, then I kind of take that as a sign from God.

The first time I ever did this strategy it worked perfectly in Costa Rica and since then it has never really worked again but it was still cool. If there's not apartments for rent there, I'll start walking concentric circles. My apartment in the Dominican Republic is walking distance of the bank, grocery store, gym, beach and restaurants.

I don't like to drive, so I always target walkable towns or areas where I can easily use public transportation. I enjoy walking and one of the things I've found living abroad is that I walk a lot more than I do when I'm in America. Daily walking has improved my mental, physical, and emotional health. I do a lot of my best thinking walking and swimming and will listen to a podcast or just enjoy the stroll.

There are three distinct reasons why I don't like to drive abroad. The first is that as a foreigner living in the Dominican Republic and if I hit someone, it's going to be my fault probably when the police arrive. And whoever I hit, or the police are going to be trying to get some cash from me. That's sometimes just how it works and police in other countries can be corrupt and view foreigners as dollar signs.

The second is some countries you ride on the other side of the road, and that's something I just can't get used to. I rented a moped in Thailand and almost killed myself like four times in the first hour and ended up taking it back because my brain was just wired for the American side of the road.

The third reason is I have driven two military vehicles in Afghanistan and have run over IEDs (improvised explosive devices). When you're driving a truck and run over a few bombs it takes the joy out of driving.

Pro Tip: You always get the best deal with apartments with boots on the ground. A lot of Veterans want a place before they come, most of the time that's a bad strategy.

Landlords

There are landlords that want to rent to you and some that are hesitant. They might think you're going to skip out and go back to America and leave unpaid rent or destroy the place. They might want a long-term renter, and you might only be staying temporarily. You'll want to make sure you have paperwork handy like a copy of your passport but out in the world cash is king and apartments are often rented differently than in the states.

Renting abroad can be very different from country to country. Some countries are more formal, and some are essentially handshake agreements. My condo I'm living in right now in the Dominican Republic, I never even signed a piece of paper. An important tip is to remember renting abroad is often more negotiable than in the states. I failed to realize this initially and probably lost some money I could have kept.

You can also get an Airbnb, then form a relationship with the owner and ask for a cash, long-term deal. Or if they know any longer-term stays. This is what I did in Medellin, Colombia because I got an apartment for a week and asked the owner how much for cash for two months. She didn't have any guests for the next 50 days, so I paid a very reasonable rate for that. Now when I go to Medellin, I'll stay there, and I will get a good deal because she trusts me.

Some Airbnb owners are open to renting their place out long term for the right guests. You can ask, they can say no, or they might quote you a high price and you can negotiate. When I rented my apartment out, I only allowed week stays and more because it's a pain to turn it over and it saved me on cleaning costs. Eventually I stopped putting my apartment on Airbnb when I travelled because people are terrible and they would steal my silverware and towels and toilet paper.

Furnished and unfurnished can mean different things in other countries. There can be different standards, and some places will be called furnished but will only have bare necessities and unfurnished apartments might not even have a stove, kitchen, fridge or other things you might expect. When you're renting make sure you know what you're getting. I'd never rent sight unseen. Facebook is an increasingly popular way to rent mid to long term apartments.

Expat Bubbles

Some people want to live around other expats, and some want a more local experience. I'm a fan of a mixed community. I don't want to feel like I'm only surrounded by Americans but don't want to be on the other end of the spectrum either. There are a lot of areas in the world with no expats if you want to be the only American around, but that makes things a little more difficult because it's not set up for expat life. The Dominican Republic has a lot of expats, but most of us are in certain areas where the infrastructure is better and there's beach access.

John's Top 10 Countries For Veterans

- Philippines
- Mexico
- Dominican Republic
- Costa Rica
- Thailand
- Colombia
- Japan
- Panama
- Germany

- Brazil

I haven't been everywhere yet, but I'm planning on traveling more in the next few years and will be writing about my experiences on my blog and on social media. Countries can rise and fall, sounds odd to say but I think Vietnam is going to be a new place for American Vets to retire to in coming years. I also think Eastern Europe has a lot of potential and there's affordable countries there but with things like wars, pandemics and economics - things can always change.

Countries that have friendlier visa requirements can adjust them; places can rise and fall. El Salvador used to be a place nobody would want to live, now expats are flocking there. When I think about the best countries for Veterans, to me it's places that already have an existing Veteran community. I understand wanting to live in the middle of nowhere or on a deserted island as well.

Chapter 22

Financial Mistakes To Avoid

There's a lot of financial mistakes we all make in life. Everybody wastes money they shouldn't, and we underestimate our spending. Moving abroad is one way to save money but that doesn't mean everything is always going to be cheaper. You do need to be careful abroad, especially in the technology world and avoid common pitfalls and scams that occur in the expat community. From ATMs that overcharge you to taxi drivers, we all face obstacles with our financial journey abroad.

25 mistake to avoid on your expat journey

1. Buying property you've never seen in person.
2. Not canceling subscriptions or memberships in the states.
3. Exchanging cash at the wrong places i.e. Airports.
4. Overindulging when you first move abroad.
5. Closing all your U.S. banking and credit cards at the same time.
6. Losing money on transfer and conversion fees
7. Letting an ATM convert your currency and not your home bank.

8. Not having a will or estate plan figured out.

9. Lack of an emergency budget.

10. Paying for a car in the states you aren't driving.

11. Forgetting to call banks and credit card companies before traveling.

12. Putting all your cards together and losing your wallet or purse.

13. Not getting the best international plan for your phone or getting hit with global roaming.

14. Not knowing about the tipping culture where you're going.

15. Having a credit or debit card with foreign transaction fees.

16. Overpaying taxes or underpaying taxes.

17. Thinking everything is going to be cheaper.

18. Focusing too much on the short term and ignoring the long game.

19. Forgetting about debts in America.

20. Keeping too many expenses back home, like not canceling your gym membership.

21. Dining in tourism hotspots.

22. Forgetting your banking information, pins, passwords, etc.

23. Dating the wrong person who uses you for your money.

24. Not keeping up with your credit situation, getting your identity stolen while abroad.

25. Not keeping yourself occupied in your new country and spending money for no reason.

NerdWallet: Best No Foreign Transaction Fees Credit Cards

Finance Buzz: Top No Foreign Transaction Fee Credit Cards

Ten Financial Scams To Avoid Abroad

1. In Thailand and some other countries foreigners can't own land and houses. So occasionally men will date a Thai woman and put the house in her name, once it's all built and paid for, she kicks him out. Kind of funny but still something to watch out for when it comes to dating.
2. Don't ever send money to someone overseas that you haven't met in person.
3. Be careful over public wi-fi. That information can be intercepted.
4. Juice Jacking – Someone loading malware or spyware onto public charging stations. Think of like public charging stations in train stations, you plug your phone in waiting for a train and someone steals your data.
5. The police robbing you. It's common in Mexico for example for a drug dealer to sell you drugs then tell on you to the police. Then the police will either say "pay up, or you're going to jail." That'll sound like, *"paga tu vas a ir a la carcel."*

6. Scams and cons will often front as charities. In Cambodia they have these fake orphanages where you'll think you're donating to these kids, but the kids just come by when the tourists are traveling through.

7. Sob stories: Children might approach you and say things like, *"I'm so hungry"* and *"My mother is sick."* You'll see disabled people begging and panhandling.

8. Not asking about the costs of things beforehand and then getting ripped off. This happens with taxis frequently but also at bars. Bars will often attempt to dramatically overcharge tourists, and sometimes pretty girls will work at the bar and get you to buy them overpriced drinks.

9. Traveling abroad can make your family susceptible to scams too. The Grandparent's Con is when someone calls or messages your family pretending to be you, or that you need help and to send them money. Now this is common on social media. I've had someone make fake Instagram and Facebook profiles of me and ask people to send them money.

10. ATM Withdrawal scams, where a card skimmer is installed, and your pin and account information are stolen. Use ATMS within banks, that have cameras and are well-lit.

Everyone knows not to exchange money at airports, but people still do it so obviously the message isn't getting through. I say that because financial mistakes are something we all make. Experience is often the best teacher, and no one is above making bad financial decisions.

If you want to give back when you're traveling or living abroad, do it through legitimate means. Beware certain people, charities, and groups abroad will take every dime from you if you let them. Going abroad means you have to be more careful with your money, your spending and your finances.

Chapter 23

Cost of Living Overseas

We're all painfully aware of the cost-of-living increases and inflation in the United States. The cost of living at home is a big reason why a lot of Veterans and military families choose to live abroad, for a better life at a cheaper cost. There's no real way to sugarcoat that life has gotten too expensive day to day, year after year in America.

I'll lead by saying that if you're 100% rated from the VA, you can live well in a lot of nonwestern countries around the world, without working. If you're retired from the military and have your VA benefits, you've got it made. If you have your VA benefits and work remotely, have rental properties or can create extra income like me, then you'll enjoy yourself overseas.

Average Rent in different city centers around the world (Quality 1 Bedroom)

- Chang Mai, Thailand - $375
- San Salvador, El Salvador $470
- Jaco, Costa Rica - $480
- Puerto Plata, Dominican Republic - $400
- Cebu, Philippines - $375

- Dakar, Sengal - $250

Here are some random cities around the world that I've travelled to with data populated by Wise[48]. To give you an idea of current conditions but these numbers will change over time. As always, things usually get more expensive compared to cheaper. I understand not everyone is moving abroad just for the cheaper cost of living but that's a big driver for a lot of Veterans. I don't want to find the cheapest location on earth, I still want my Western amenities like hot water and nice restaurants.

Head over to Numbeo[49] to investigate some cost-of-living information. You can use their comparison calculators where you can input your current city and where you might want to go. I prefer Numbeo because it's simple and straightforward and I've found the data to be accurate. The second cost-of-living calculator I would recommend you investigate is LivingCost.org[50] - because you can insert your current income and play with that. That's especially helpful if you plan on moving abroad with a fixed income.

---

[48] https://wise.com/gb/cost-of-living/index-by-country

[49] https://www.numbeo.com/cost-of-living/

[50] https://livingcost.org/

City comparisons are more useful than country comparisons when it comes to using these tools. The more specific you are, the better off you'll be. Which neighborhood you choose within a city impacts your prices. I like going to Medellin a lot, life is more expensive in the El Poblado neighborhood than in other districts because that's the tourist area.

If you use these tools, don't try to go to the edge of your budget. If your budget happens to be $4,000 a month, then don't move somewhere that costs $3,900 to live. Life is always pricier the first few months somewhere and these calculators obviously are not 100% accurate all the time. There is always lots of debate about prices and people lie. Expats love to brag about how little they pay, I wouldn't put much faith into online influencers.

My first ever apartment abroad was in Bangkok, Thailand and I was paying $300 a month for a beautiful apartment building with a pool, gym and amazing views. That was years ago and I'm sure that the same apartment is probably $500 or more now. As a general rule, things get more expensive and not cheaper. Everyone has a different ideal living situation and cost of living; you might be happy eating like a local in Thailand and spending $2-3 a meal. Or you might want Netflix and Spotify subscriptions, gym memberships and an international phone plan.

How much money you need overseas is a different question and answer for everyone. One of the things that I enjoy about living abroad is I can go out to dinner more and drink the good stuff for a better price. If I cooked at home all month, it would be a big money saver. If I ate the local Dominican chicken and rice every day, I'd spend hardly any money on food. I know Veterans that pinch pennies and live like monks, here in the Dominican Republic and in other countries and that isn't really for me. You know yourself, you know if you're happy sitting at home watching TV and reading most evenings or if you're going to be going out on the town.

Some veterans end up spending roughly the same as they do in the states because they live a higher quality life. If you live in Mexico you might decide to have a pool, a maid, and go out to eat all the time. A lot of veterans still will have expenses in the states whether it's debt, storage, child support, or whatever else. Having a higher quality of life at a lower price is a big benefit of moving abroad but for me it's also about the peace my life abroad provides.

Chapter 24

GI Bill Abroad

More and more Veterans are seeing the appeal of either using their GI Bill online while living abroad or attending foreign institutions. If you've got an internet connection, then you can utilize your GI Bill benefits anywhere in the world to get an online education, and more and more degrees are only online. You're going to get the same BAH going to school online no matter where you live, and all you need is your laptop.

The GI Bill is one of the best benefits that we receive, and a lot of Veterans never take advantage of it. Some Vets look at going to college like it isn't for us, that's why we joined the military. I felt like that when I got out of the military, I had already failed out of community college before joining the military. My first college class using my GI Bill in my thirties had me feeling like I crash landed on another planet. My M4 was gone, and my environment went from infantry guys in camouflage to kids with iPhone and Starbucks cups.

There are lots of different ways to go to college nowadays and the GI Bill is more flexible then ever. The GI Bill isn't contained to your local community college, it's a worldwide benefit. A lot of schools around the world will happily receive your GI Bill dollars straight from our government, they know they're getting paid the full tuition rate. There are many institutions around the world who advertise and market their programs to Veteran students. It's for two reasons, one is economics, they get paid a lot every semester you're there and the second is that we're good students. We show up on time, do our assignments and are respectful.

I'm going to walk you through step by step your options going to school in a different country, how to do it, BAH rates and everything you need to know. We live in a digital world, and it goes without saying that you've got two ways to go to school, online and in person. I'll cover the online portion first because that's simple and you can go to a US based school.

School Online

You can use the GI Bill for lots of online programs, independent learning and virtual courses. The downside to going to school online is that your Basic Allowance for Housing (BAH) comes in at half of the national average. This number fluctuates but usually goes up year after year. As of this writing, the current amount is $1,177.50 which is half of the national average of an E-5 with dependents. This is going to be if you're taking zero classes in person, meaning you can take these classes from anywhere in the world. In addition to the monthly allowance, you can also receive your book stipends and fees.

This can be a great way to not only get an education but also supplement your income. If you're making an extra thousand bucks a month, life is better. Veterans tend to steer clear of online education more than most, we prefer real world, experiential learning. That's what the military is, you can't learn to shoot a rifle or work a radio without touching either of them in person.

We live in an increasingly technological world, and you receive the same degree if you go in person or not. Going to class a few hours a week while on a beach somewhere isn't the worst life. Online education requires a little more discipline and to be a self-starter as well as some technological skills.

In Person

Going to a foreign school in person can present a few unique challenges. But you're not the first Veteran to do it. Going to school abroad presents a lot of great learning opportunities, travel and real-world education. Not enough Veterans take advantage of this opportunity, and I want to get the word out about schools that do a great job with Veterans abroad. It's absolutely best to go to a school who has already had Veterans there and understands the GI Bill.

Step 1

- Select the country you want to go to school in and search the GI Bill approved schools there.

Find a GI Approved School by Country

https://inquiry.vba.va.gov/weamspub/buildSearchCou

ntryCriteria.do

Keep in mind, just because the government approves the school doesn't mean the school knows what the hell they are doing when it comes to Veteran students. Some schools on the lists won't know the process and since the government takes a while to pay your tuition, you can run into problems. The best strategy is to find the school you want to go to and then search their website for a VA representative.

If they don't have one listed, contact them to see. If you're still confused, email federal.approvals@va.gov with the schools name, address and program information. An important thing to know is just because the GI Bill approves of the school, doesn't mean they cover that program. When it comes to schools abroad, both the school and the specific degree program or courses must be approved by the VA.

Step 2

You get your certificate of eligibility (COE) just like you would in the states. You can visit the VA website and *"apply for educational benefits."* That's the easiest method and you can download or get your certificate emailed to you. Your second option is to apply by mail. You would download the application, VA Form 22-1990 and mail it to the address listed on the form, you can download it easily online.

Your third option is to do it by phone, call the VA educational center and they'll email or send one to you. It can take the VA a little bit of time to process your COE, so don't do it right before you have to start a foreign school.

It's your responsibility to get this document to your school and then they handle the rest. The next step is only available to on campus reps, but they can only do it after they receive your Certificate of Eligibility. They submit your enrollment to the VA with a 22-1999 form and the VA will certify you at that institution. This is why it's best to attend an institution that already has and understands Veterans. Honestly, if the school has no idea how to handle your enrollment, I'd move on and pick a different institution abroad.

Step 3

Figure out the individual visa situation, go to class, kick ass, have a good time and graduate.

BAH

The abroad BAH rate is a flat rate. This confuses a lot of Veterans because we're used to a BAH rate being dependent on your zip code. Because it's a flat rate, it makes sense to try to attend a school in a country with a low cost of living. Somewhere like the Philippines comes to mind opposed to somewhere like Switzerland. That doesn't mean you need to go somewhere with a cheap cost of living, but you want your BAH to cover your housing costs.

The current rate is $2,338 for 2025-2026 but will go up or down the following year depending on worldwide economics. Again, it's going to be that much no matter where you go in the world, from Canada to China to Australia to Argentina. It's all the same, you still get the same book stipend you would in the United States. Keep in mind, it often takes two calendar months to kick in so plan accordingly.

If you do go to school abroad, in the states, online or use your GI Bill at all - check out my book Combat To College[51] and my Student Veteran Semester Planner[52]. They are both available on Amazon and my website and I also have a Free Student Veteran Coaching Program[53] I developed as well.

I dropped out of community college, or failed out is probably more accurate and ended up in an Army Recruiters office. When I got out of the military, I realized school was actually pretty easy if you just showed up and did the work. I ended up going to Harvard for my master's degree and even pitched legislation to congress about student Veteran issues. You earned your GI Bill, you should use it.

---

[51] https://a.co/d/fggiozx - Amazon Link for Combat To College

[52] https://a.co/d/fqkmexX - Amazon Link For Student Vet Semester Planner

[53] https://www.johnhdaviswriter.com/the-combat-to-college-grow-method/

Chapter 25

Learning The Language

My first living abroad experience was in Thailand and I walked out of my first Thai class after approximately fifteen minutes. I knew I wasn't going to stick it out and become fluent in Thai, it's a hard language for Americans to learn. One reason was because speaking Thai is pretty much only useful in Thailand. There are a lot of languages that have worldwide value, Thai does not. If I would have been committed to living in Thailand for the rest of my life, I would have put more effort in, but I knew I wouldn't be there forever.

I learned or tried to learn a few Thai greetings and how to say please and thank you and that was pretty much it. When I started learning Spanish, I knew I was going to stick with it because Spanish is useful in over twenty countries plus back in America. English is always the best language to know, it's the language of worldwide business and entertainment and no matter where you go, you'll always find someone who speaks English. Lots of Americans prefer to move places like Jamaica or Australia where everyone already speaks English, it makes life easier when you remove the language barrier.

The first real experience I had in Thailand talking to people was in my hostel. I had just landed and caught a taxi there from the airport and I walk in and there's a group of people at the bar. I thought after a 24-hour travel situation that a beer sounded pretty good, so I wandered up there and was surprised to hear everyone speaking English. It was everyone's second language, there was a couple there from Germany, a guy from Russia, a girl from India and a Thai bartender and they all were communicating in somewhat decent English. How else would they communicate? Obviously, the Indian person didn't speak German or Russian or Thai. This gave me a sense of confidence traveling because pretty much all foreign travelers speak a little bit of English, no matter where they call home.

It might be because we're too stubborn to learn another language, so the rest of the world has to accommodate us or because we're a superpower or because our culture is so strong. You can head into the deepest reaches of Africa, and you'll see someone with a NBA jersey on and everyone in the world knows who the President of the United States is. Everyone has seen the Avengers, and everyone knows who 50 Cent is.

If You're Serious

If you're serious about it, you can learn any language. I believe that because I've seen it with our Veteran population. I've met Veterans who fell in love with a girl in South Korea while being stationed there and now speak fluent Korean. I've met Veterans who have at fifty years old learned Spanish, Portuguese, Chinese and more. I kind of stumbled into trying to learn Spanish and never really had a formal strategy to it. The best lessons I've had have been just living in a foreign country.

The apps I've had success with are Babell and Duolingo, there are other options out there and Rosetta Stone offers at least 10% off to Veterans. I have paid for Babbell and that's been useful for me. I personally prefer to do my language lessons on my computer and not my phone but Duolingo is great on your phone as well. You're on your phone more than you should be already; you might as well do something useful with that time. A lot of Veterans are hesitant to pay for something, I paid, and it was worth it to me. They run specials a lot but it's not very expensive and you can do your lessons on your own time.

Initially, I started learning Spanish to talk to Dominican girls. When I committed to staying in the Dominican Republic long term I started practicing for everyday life. Dating is a pretty good way to learn a new language, every date is like a lesson and you learn as you go. If you're married or don't want to date, then switch your Netflix over to your target language. There are also tons of YouTube resources, and I even bought Spanish flashcards.

I started out really shy with my Spanish, I didn't want to sound dumb. I knew I was messing words and conjugations up and it took a little bit to get over that. A lot of Veterans tend to judge themselves overly harshly when learning a new language, we're hard on ourselves and our mistakes. We shouldn't be because part of learning a new language is butchering it. I still speak Spanish sort of terribly but if my point gets across then I'm satisfied. There's no test involved.

Don't start off on your language journey aiming for perfection. My Spanish will never be as good as a native speaker probably and I'm okay with that. A lot of people will be delighted to help you learn and won't be critical. It's not about being perfectly fluent, it's about communicating. The people in your new country will be very happy you're trying to learn, a lot of expats don't bother. Even learning 10 phrases means a lot to people and everyday language, the stuff you'll need to say isn't that complicated.

Best 10 Phrases To Learn

1. *Hello/ Please/ Thank you*
2. *How much is this?*
3. *Can you repeat that?*
4. *My name is...*
5. *Where is the bathroom?*
6. *Directional language: Right, left, straight, stop, etc*
7. *Numbers*

8. *I am sorry/ Excuse me.*
9. *I need help.*
10. *How do you say...*

People are far kinder and more accepting of your language attempts than you might think. If you think to your own experiences with foreigners in America, I'm sure you aren't' like *"That's not how you say that idiot!"* Plus, lots of people want to learn English so language exchange is a popular thing to do. Start off with learning these ten phrases and go from there.

Myth 1- I can never learn another language.

Some people are better at languages than others, like some people are better at shooting basketball than others. You can absolutely do it if you commit yourself. Even a half commitment will help you out and once you get some momentum it feels good.

Myth 2- I can't move to a country because I can't speak the language.

People move to America all the time without knowing English and pick it up. The best way to learn is to move and start speaking. You can go abroad with English and be confident. You don't need to be fluent in a second language to move abroad.

Myth 3- I'm too old to learn a new language

Veterans should embrace lifelong learning. I accept the research that says it's easier to learn a new language younger, but a lot of things are easier when you're younger like running a marathon or touching your toes. You aren't too old to pick it up.

English is so widely spoken you'll find it one of the languages in over forty countries. Having an American passport and speaking English is a big leg up in the travel world. Younger people everywhere want to speak English, and the American dream might have lost some of its shine for us but for a lot of people abroad it's very much alive. I tell people who are moving here to the Dominican Republic, "YOU SPEAK ENGLISH! LOTS OF PEOPLE SPEAK ENGLISH HERE!" It's not like you're moving here only speaking Korean, then you might have some problems. No matter where you go, someone will be speaking our language and especially in the expat type areas.

English Speaking Countries

- *USA*
- *Antigua*
- *Australia*
- *Bahamas*
- *Barbados*
- *Belize*

- *Bermuda*
- *Botswana*
- *Canada*
- *Caymen Islands*
- *Dominica*
- *Fiji*
- *Gambia*
- *Ghana*
- *India*
- *Ireland*
- *Jamaica*
- *Kenya*
- *Lesotho*
- *Liberia*
- *Malawi*
- *Malta*
- *New Zealand*
- *Nigeria*
- *Papua New Guinea*
- *The Philippines*
- *South Africa*
- *Trinidad and Tobago*
- *United Kingdom*

I have a friend in the Dominican Republic who's a little older and initially refused to learn any Spanish. He said, "I'm never going to understand it so why bother?" I said "sure, maybe not but why not just learn five phrases to use in your everyday life and go from there." He found out people were so delighted when he used his phrases that he learned a little more, then a little more and now he's doing great.

Learning the language in your new country will help you meet people, it'll assist your cultural understanding, and it'll help you assimilate. I've spoken to a lot of people who don't want to move abroad because they don't speak the language. You move, then you learn. Or you don't, it's your decision. You can also select one of the above countries where English is one of the languages then you don't need to worry about it, or in certain expat areas it really doesn't matter.

The simple act of communication requires a sender and a receiver, if you're doing that then you're communicating. That's a start and you can learn a little at a time. Google translate will likely be your best friend and there's a lot of great technology resources to learn a new language. It seems like in a few years we'll all have computer chips in our heads or something so that'll help. Use every resource at your disposal, don't be afraid to spend a few bucks, take formal classes or go at it on your own. You can meet a lot of fellow expats in language classes as well and they are worth taking.

Living abroad puts you in a position where you have to use the language to some extent. I can order pizza to my condo in the Dominican Republic with an app or I can call the restaurant. I can negotiate a taxi on my own or I can just use Uber. I can pass a phone to someone with a google translate phrase or I can try to make it on my own. There are a lot of options and learning the language will help you a lot in your new country. My Spanish isn't great, but by the time you read this hopefully it'll be a bit better.

Chapter 26

Family Life

When I first started getting messages on social media and emails from Veterans interested in living abroad, I was surprised how many families were interested. I assumed the majority of Veterans wanting to move abroad would be single and primarily male, but I started getting a lot of families and female vets that wanted to explore the idea. A lot of families like the idea of spending more time together, getting their kids an international education or even homeschooling.

I've advised families of five move to Costa Rica and dual military couples who want to backpack SE Asia. There are a lot of quality schools abroad, I've personally taught in Thailand, Cambodia and worked in educational environments in Senegal. My master's degree is in international education and for a while I wanted to work in refugee camps and conflict education after my experiences in Afghanistan.

A family I recently talked to just wanted a slower paced life, they realized they were running around and missing their kids growing up. They weren't getting special moments because everything was go-go-go for them and their kids. Then they moved to Mexico, and they eat meals together, play together and disconnected from the United States. Their kids are learning Spanish, which is better than learning Algebra nowadays. Many international schools offer far superior educational experiences for your kids than American public schools.

Moving abroad with a family is a growing, learning and challenging experience. You'll come together as a family, even if it's through shared obstacles. My friend David lives here in the Dominican Republic as a single father with his two sons. For him, he wanted the freedom to raise his kids more how he wanted and less what he saw in Atlanta.

"My kids aren't glued to their screens here, they still love playing video games but it's not a 24/7 seven thing. They want to be outside, playing and running around."

When kids are involved, the stakes are higher. I know it's more stressful and more involved. Military kids are usually resilient and good at adapting, but it isn't always easy. Usually, the kids transition better abroad than their parents because it's easy for them to make friends in schools, clubs, parks and more. They jump right into the swing of things and are less cautious and more curious but of course it's not always like that.

Kids usually adapt to the native language quicker, but it still isn't easy. They are going to miss things about home like you will and kids always don't understand or can't emotionally comprehend the move abroad. Kids aren't as concerned with the cost of living, taxes and the adult shit that we preoccupy ourselves with.

Cons To Family Life Abroad

- There's no automatic way to know how your kids will adjust.
- Languages are hard for everyone.
- Introverted kids can struggle abroad without extended family.
- Your kids can resent you if they don't want to move.
- Potential academic disruption moving into a different system.
- They might resist cultural adjustments.
- If you're kids are picky eaters or overly used to American style foods.

Moving abroad with kids of different ages is obviously far different. Taking a sixteen-year-old abroad is a lot different than a two-year-old. One of the important things when it comes to taking kids abroad is to make it a collaborative effort. Bring them into the discussion as early as possible, even when it comes to the planning phases because this is a family move. The more involved they feel and the more agency they feel the better they will handle the transition process.

The parents are often heavily involved in the actual logistics of the move and not the emotions of it. Those are kind of two different things and children experience the emotional aspect differently. You're probably more excited, they aren't sure how to feel. It can be a complicated process and even though they might seem pumped up about it, they have unspoken emotions. You'll want to encourage conversations about it.

Expat teens can have serious concerns, teenagers are already crazy and experiencing hormonal transitions. When you toss in a totally new culture, new language and a new country it can be a disaster. They can withdraw or rebel or throw themselves into bad behavior. I was a crazy ass teenager in my hometown without moving to a new land. It's much harder moving abroad with teenagers than little kids.

Sometimes the best strategy is to wait until your kids get on their own to move abroad, to go off to college or join the military themselves. I know several Veteran parents now that are waiting for their kids to finish up school and start their own lives before moving abroad. Taking a few teenagers abroad can be a daunting experience and every kid reacts to moving abroad differently but you know your kids better than anyone.

Teenage Tips

Don't go home too soon to visit after moving.

Try to keep routines similar.

Try to keep familiarity, even small things like the same framed photos, food, or pillow.

Don't drag them kicking and screaming to a new country.

Let them find their own way as much as possible and encourage curiosity.

Teenagers are going to be teenagers, some problems are normal no matter where you are in the world.

Expat Child Syndrome

Expat Child Syndrome, or ECS is a term coined by psychologists to describe the stress and difficult emotional adjustments children can have when moving abroad. These manifest with things like withdrawal, defiance, behavioral changes or other symptoms. They might move to a new place and not fit in, they might be a different color than everyone else and speak a different language. They might have grown up playing baseball and moved to a place where everyone plays soccer and it's just a difficult transition.

Everyone responds differently to moving abroad, when it comes to kids they might sleep too much or too little, depression, mood swings or none of the above. I think a lot of parents overly expect their kids to transition perfectly abroad and are surprised when they encounter challenges. Parenting is tough no matter where you are in the world.

Pros To Family Life Abroad

- Your kids will become bilingual.
- No school shooting concerns.
- Less social pressure.
- Less politics at a younger age.
- Youth mental health can improve.
- Opportunities for less processed foods.
- More family friendly culture.
- Educational cultural experiences.

Finding International Schools

Finding an educational school in certain environments can be a daunting experience. Every parent wants the best for their child and where you move might be dependent on where you can find a good school. In my little area in the Dominican Republic, there's only one international school so it's kind of an easy choice if you move here.

In bigger cities like Bangkok, Thailand, there are lots of quality international schools to choose from. Pretty much all nice areas abroad will have quality international schools where all the expat kids as well as the wealthier local kids will go to. If you're looking for a new place to live in your city, asking the school ideal neighborhoods or where the other kids go can be a big help.

I've toured schools when I've visited other countries and usually, they offer a more holistic and personal education. Class sizes are smaller, there's less focus on sports, more music and language instruction. Your kids also have the benefit of going to school with kids from different countries. To use my area again for an example, we have an expat population of Americans, Germans, Russians, Canadians and a Jewish population so the school is diverse. The international school I taught at in Cambodia was 95% Cambodian kids and the school here in the Dominican Republic is 95% foreign kids.

In foreign countries, sometimes the public educational system is good like in Costa Rica and South Korea and sometimes it's bad. I wouldn't send my kids to a public school in the Dominican Republic probably, but I also probably wouldn't send my kids to a lot of schools in American cities. My kids don't exist, so it's not really a current concern. But I still talk to a lot of Veteran expats with kids and most of them have been incredibly satisfied with their kids' education abroad and how life offers a lot of opportunities for growth and learning.

Expatica: Finding A School Program In A New Country[54]

---

[54]   https://www.expatica.com/global/education/children-education/finding-a-school-abroad-104478/

Fast Facts About International Schools

- The primary language will usually be English.
- The more expensive, usually the better.
- International schools will be accredited, so no problems with degrees or college.

International schools will often focus more on setting kids on a good path for international business and the globalized economy. A lot of expat kids will move around the world in the future, so they want to set them up for worldwide success. Students are often held to a high standard and there are less discipline issues. I did my student teaching in the United States, and I was pretty shocked at the behavior and vulgarity of seventh graders. I had never been cursed at by a kid before and I was straight out of the Army, so I struggled with that.

One of the things I noticed when it came to comparing my teaching experiences in public schools in New York versus abroad is that abroad it felt like the parents, teachers and administrators were more on the same page. I was teaching in a classy private school in Thailand, but in US public schools it felt like the parents and school administration had a more combative relationship with classroo teachers.

International private schools are often more passionate about their students' college success. They base a lot of their business around being able to tell prospective parents that a certain number went to Ivy League colleges or top tier schools. They want to make sure kids graduating have open doors and opportunities. Whereas public schools sometimes don't care. Public school education in foreign countries differs as much as it does in the states. Some areas are great, some underfunded and some terrible.

It's hard to give general advice when it comes to public schools abroad, but you'll have an idea if you'd be willing to put your kids in there or not. Public schools' language of instruction will obviously be the language of the country. If you want to move to a Spanish speaking country and your kids already speak Spanish, putting them in a public school makes more sense.

I recognize it was a hell of a lot easier for me to move abroad as a single guy than with a family. It can be hard to imagine how kids are going to handle the transition, will they struggle or thrive? Change is a big deal for families and kids and presents real challenges. Having your kids as involved as possible can go a long way. You might be going back and forth trying to decide if you're making the best decisions for your family. If you frame the whole experience as fun and an adventure, then even the tough times won't feel as bad. Because there's always difficult moments in every adventure story and fairy tale.

Kids are visual creatures so show them pictures and videos of where you're going. Brand new shit to kids can be intimidating. Let them explore on YouTube. Make it real for them and let them make some of the decisions, ask them what they think about this or that. Let them decorate the new house or choose where you eat or even what flight to take. Let them feel like grownups at times and like kids at times.

Incorporate as many of your family routines into your new home as possible, if you always read a story to your kid before bed then make sure you continue to do that. If they love a certain movie, make sure they can watch it on the computer or something. There's plenty of information out there about moving abroad as a family, lots of videos and lots of advice. No matter how much preparation you put into moving abroad, it's never perfectly smooth so don't expect it to be.

Locations differ a lot when it comes to visas, schooling and family life. Connect with other families that have moved abroad and are living in your location. Get on Facebook groups and expat message boards to find kid friendly activities in your area and connect with other parents. Your kids can sometimes be your best asset because they'll meet kids at school, and you'll meet the parents. The international school can sometimes be the best resource because they'll have things like orientation nights, local assistance and more because often they have lots of expat parents.

Chapter 27

The Bureaucracy

The most annoying part of moving abroad is the most annoying aspect of anything, the paperwork. There are legalities, visa applications, waiting times and red tape. When you first start to look into moving abroad it can seem to be a bit much, every place has different requirements, and some are harder than others. Every country has their own unique system for longer term stays and there are no universal policies.

In the most basic sense, a visa is what gives you permission to enter or stay in a specific country for a period of time. There are many different types of visas, and they change frequently. One reason I chose the Dominican Republic over other places is that it's easier than most places to stay long term. We are lucky as Americans that a lot of countries grant us long stays with tourist visas, you can stay in Mexico six months without worrying about applying for anything. But even as an American, with an American passport, you can be deported. Americans getting deported to me is always kind of funny and I've seen Americans get deported for overstaying visas, petty crime and drug use.

You're going to want to stay on the right side of immigration laws and cross every T and dot every I. Most places are looking for expats who are going to benefit their country and spend their money there. Nowhere else besides our nation has a sign that reads, *"Give me your tired, your poor, your huddled masses yearning to breathe free, The wretched refuse of your teeming shore."* Other nations want to know if you're going to be a burden or an asset. For a lot of countries that means the most important thing is money.

Some countries have higher income thresholds for visas and some lower, depending on where you want to go. They're happy if you're eating out, partying, and throwing your American dollars around. A lot of nations will want to make sure you have the cash and want to see bank statements and steady income whether that's pension information or a regular paycheck.

What You Might Need

Criminal Background Check: Nobody wants murderers and rapists within their borders, a lot of places will want to make sure you aren't wanted and haven't been found guilty of major crimes.

Health Insurance: Certain countries will want to make sure if you get very sick, they're not on the hook for your treatment.

Vaccinations: In certain countries you'll be required to show your vaccinated against certain things. Some places require shots Americans don't traditionally get such as the Yellow Fever vaccine.

Making it easier

Money greases the wheels of everything. A lot of countries have citizenship by investment, or if you park a certain amount of cash in their banking system. Citizenship by investment is what it sounds, you buy a house, or a business and they know you have money, so they want you there. If you've got some deep pockets, you can go about anywhere, nobody turns down cash. The more money you have, the less problems you'll have in your visa process and the less money you have the more obstacles you'll face. A lot of countries have rules where if you park a certain amount of cash in their banks without touching it for a period or keep your balance over a certain amount they'll grant you a visa.

Visas

The biggest challenge in any expat's life can be figuring out the visa process and staying somewhere legally. A visa gives you legal permission to stay in a country for a set amount of time and for a specific reason. It serves as a permit to enter a country for a specific reason and can include duration of stay, whether you're allowed to work, and more countries are opting for electronic visas.

Tourist

This is where I always recommend people to start. You're not supposed to work in most places when you're on a tourist visa, but obviously people do, especially online. You want to at least visit initially on a tourist visa before making any permanent moves. Most tourist visas require you to have an onward or return ticket. Get one you can adjust or cancel without losing money or roll the dice. They might ask for one when you board the flight or arrive in the other country or they might not.

Work

There's no cookie cutter, international standard when it comes to work visas. The requirements everywhere are different, and it depends on what your employment is. I had a work visa for teaching English in Thailand, it was pretty straightforward, and the school helped me out with the necessary paperwork. They basically did it all for me. Most countries, unless it's a foreign company, lean away from hiring expats and some have to show why they are hiring you and not a local person.

If you have exceptional skills, from engineering to being an incredible artist, it can be easier to land a visa. The United States give these based on *"exceptional ability"* which is how often celebrities or entertainers end up with an easy visa process. The reality is if someone hires you overseas, they usually have to prove that they can't hire someone domestically for your role. If a local could do your job, then a lot of governments have rules that it has to go to them. Exceptions are things like chefs, teachers, and highly technical roles.

Working Holiday Visa

This is traditionally designed for younger people to work within a country for a set period of time, usually a year. Think of it like a study abroad program, but you're working. Lots of seasonal jobs hire foreigners on holiday visas but this is mainly for young people who are looking to travel and work.

There's also working holiday programs that you can join that streamline the process for you. There aren't many countries where Americans can do Working Holiday's because they're usually based around reciprocal agreements. As of now, Australia, Singapore, South Korea, New Zealand, Ireland and Canada are on the list for Americans but that might be different by the time you read this.

Resources

- Globalworkandtravel.com
- https://welcometo.travel/
- Bunac.org

Freelancer Visa

There are a lot of countries to choose from that offer freelancing visas and they're often adjusting requirements. This is for individuals that are self-employed, and most freelance visas are valid for a few months to a couple years. For example, Spain currently offers a freelance visa if you can show you're making $3,500 a month, Brazil is $1,500, Argentina $500 and Costa Rica $2,500 as of this writing.

Freelancers and digital nomads aren't always the same thing, a freelancer is usually self-employed, and a digital nomad might work for a certain company. Freelance visas usually change more than other types because they're newer and countries are introducing them and adjusting the requirements.

Education

Studying abroad isn't just for kids; education is a lifelong endeavor. If you have the opportunity to formally study abroad, go for it. Being a student also plugs you directly into a community, provides structure, and is a great way to meet people. It can also lead you to a work visa and help you network within the country if you decide to stay long-term.

If you're an academic, studying something or teaching can make the visa process easier if you're working with or for an academic institution. But like anything, there's ways around things for example Thailand offers a self-defense visa if you're taking Muay Thai or fitness classes.

Retirement/Pension

A lot of countries will refer to a retirement visa as a pension visa. You'll need to demonstrate that you earn a certain amount of money monthly from your retirement and that differs country to country.

In Latvia it's $1,125 dollars a month and in Dubai over $5,000. Countries can also have age requirements to quality for any retirement options and those can change over time. Thailand's minimum retirement age is fifty whereas Costa Rica has no minimum retirement age. As veterans we tend to retire earlier so I would look into retirement age restrictions in your ideal countries. This is one of the most popular options for Veterans.

Note: Some countries are happy to treat your VA benefits as a pension. You might need to get a letter from a VA counselor to accompany your benefits letter.

Retirement visas are generally what other countries want from their expats. You're spending money there and not working so you aren't taking away employment from anyone else. It's generally seen as a positive thing from other nations, they want your dollars. A military, police, or similar retirement will qualify you to live in a lot of different countries and those steady dollars will provide you with a high quality life. Or at least a higher quality life than they would in the United States.

Digital Nomad

A digital nomad is someone that works remotely outside their home country using technology. This is getting popular, because if you're solely working from your computer then you'd probably rather be on a beach somewhere. These are popular with younger people who are into slow travel and don't plan on staying anywhere forever.

Around fifty countries offer some type of digital nomad option and will run you anywhere from like $150 to $2,000 to get one. A digital nomad job is location-independent and generally more flexible. Some jobs will not permit you to work abroad so check with your employer if you're working remotely. The digital nomad movement is a product of our time, a brand-new demographic of humans working remotely and taking advantage of Geo arbitrage. The income a Digital Nomad receives is earned outside of the country they are residing in.

5 Things to Know about Digital Nomad Visas

- Income requirements vary from country to country.
- You need to have a job you can do from anywhere.
- There can be tax implications depending on your location. You might get double taxed.

- Different time zones can throw a wrench into things.
- You can do digital nomad visas with family as well.

Purchase Citizenship or Golden Visas

As you have no doubt figured out by now, money makes life a lot simpler, and you can add citizenship to the things you can buy with a credit card. Some of these places are going to require things like a clean criminal record and for you to demonstrate you didn't make your money in an ill-gotten manner.

The upper levels of the rich might buy foreign citizenship for tax reasons. You can also get citizenship through real estate or business investment. Some countries even allow you to purchase government bonds to earn a visa or citizenship. This can be a fast path to long-term citizenship but just buying property in a foreign country doesn't automatically mean you get a visa or citizenship.

Missionary/Religious

If you'd like to go spread the good word, of whatever religion you engage in then a religious visa might work. Usually, you'd do this through an international religious organization, the Mormons are famous for going abroad on religious missions. Some mission organizations have age restrictions and usually want younger people.

International Mission Organizations

• World Race[55]

• World Missions Alliance[56]

• Send International[57]

Dual Citizenship

If you're interested in getting a second passport or dual citizenship that doesn't necessarily mean you need to give up your American passport. You can still vote in the US elections and yes, you can still pay your taxes. Lucky you.

There are more types of visas and lots of countries are offering more attractive visas every year. Once you narrow down where you might like to live, you'll have to see which visa type appeals to you. You might even use several different visa types during your stay. Don't be intimidated by the process, it's like paperwork in the military - it's a pain in the ass but there's no way to avoid it.

---

[55] https://www.worldrace.org/

[56] https://rfwma.org/

[57] https://www.send.org/

Chapter 28

Safety Abroad

It might not seem like it when you look at the news and social media but the world today is a lot safer than it's ever been. There's less violent deaths, wars, famine and diseases. But safety is a top concern of a lot of travelers and Vets interested in moving abroad. It might surprise you how safer other places feel than our country. American cities have become almost like the third world in some places, we lose more Americans to drugs and violence than we ever did during the War On Terror.

Similar to as in the states, violence abroad is usually contained to specific areas. Friends and family are going to think you're walking some tight rope of death moving abroad. Maybe at any instant you'll be kidnapped or killed. Half of my friends and family probably thought I'd be dead or have some tragic event occur to me abroad. Thus far, nothing. I feel far safer living in the Dominican Republic than I do when I visit major American cities. One thing that's sure to decrease when you move abroad is your risk of getting shot.

People will assume you're rich because you're an American abroad and compared to a lot of them, you probably are. You can be a target for pickpockets and scam artists and that's more of a financial risk than physical danger. One aspect that rings true about American crime and violence is the randomness of it, it feels like anything can happen at any time. I know there's not going to be a school shooting here in the Dominican Republic, because that just doesn't happen here.

Crime occurs everywhere, corruption exists everywhere, and bad people are everywhere. A lot of people go abroad or take a vacation and act in ways they would never act in their city. If you wouldn't do it at home, don't do it abroad. Don't put yourself in risky positions and obviously don't break the law. Being too drunk is never a good idea but the good Lord knows I've had my share of drunk nights around the world. When I'm planning on going out and enjoying some nightlife, I always wear zippered pockets, I never take more cash than I'm planning on spending, and I usually have friends with me.

If I'm going out by myself, I make sure to not be walking around obliviously looking at my phone and I make sure to watch my drinks, look out for threats and keep myself aware. As Veterans, we know how to take care of ourselves, do recon and have an escape route. It's pretty much the same things you do when you go out in the United States but you do need to take increased precautions.

Where I live in the Dominican Republic is incredibly safe but there are areas nearby that aren't. When you look up news abroad, or see some American tourist killed somewhere remember the old adage *"if it bleeds, it leads."* Bad news always makes the headlines. I'm usually surprised when people tell me they don't leave the resorts in the Dominican Republic, what's the point of coming then? I don't want to blame the victims of crimes but if you're drunk at three in the morning and going to some bad neighborhood to meet a girl from Tinder in Colombia then you're putting yourself in harm's way.

When I was in Costa Rica a girl attempted to pickpocket me while another girl distracted me. Things like that happen, that's why I wear zippered pockets. They didn't even care that I caught them, they probably pay off the bouncers to work the crowd. I've also seen a team where one person spilled a drink on the tourist and the other person disappeared with the person's bag. But in my mind, I thought that they shouldn't have just put their bag on the ground behind them like that. If you put yourself in bad positions, bad things can happen. I've never been attacked, stabbed, drugged or had any issues in years of traveling.

Safety Tips

- Keep your wits about you, don't be drunk in strange places.

- Don't walk around flashing cash or a new fancy iPhone.
- Resist walking around with headphones on, it can make you less aware.
- Walk with your bag away from the street, so no one can snatch it driving.

Top 10 Safest Countries

- Singapore
- Iceland
- Denmark
- Finland
- Switzerland
- Norway
- Austria
- Sweden
- Ireland
- Japan

The 10 Most Dangerous Places To Live

- Somalia
- Yemen
- Afghanistan
- Sudan
- Haiti
- Mali

- Chad
- Congo
- Niger
- Libya

You should trust your gut instincts when it comes to safety, if something feels off then it probably is. You can buy a money belt if it feels better. Lots of travelers wear them and there are some good ones out there. Don't put all your credit cards together because if you lose them, you'll lose all of them. Don't walk around with your passport and don't trust strangers who seem too nice.

Safety Tips

- Don't look like you're lost. Be confident and alert.
- Only use ATMs that feel secure or within banks.
- Don't wear expensive jewelry.
- Only use official taxis or transportation.
- Check maps beforehand to become familiar with an area.
- Travel with someone when possible.
- Find up to date safety tips from people in the area.
- Understand exchange rates so you don't get ripped off.
- Get portable chargers if you're traveling for long periods of time.

People are often worried about someone stealing their passport, but honestly passports aren't really stolen much.

Because what is someone going to do with an American passport with your face and information on it? There's not going to be any *Mission Impossible* stuff where they wear a mask of your face and sneak into the United States.

People are more likely to steal your cell phone than anything else, because that's valuable and they might be able to get your data if you don't have it properly safeguarded. The one exception to the rule is the police, if a corrupt police officer gets your passport, he or she will definitely charge you to get it back. Don't give copies of your passport up to anyone, have a digital or paper copy for everything abroad. Money, phone and passport are your most sensitive items. Protect all of them.

Chapter 29

Mental Health Abroad

Self-care becomes more important abroad and I mean that in every sense possible. Physical, mental, emotional, and even your spiritual health are all things to give serious consideration to. Living abroad calls for you to take more personal responsibility for your mental health situation.

You might not have certain support networks, friends and family. The same resources for Veterans don't exist overseas. There are unique and specific mental health challenges that come along with moving and living abroad that are vital to prepare for and expect. There are two main dangers when it comes to Veterans moving abroad, first is the risk of isolation and second the exacerbation of PTSD.

Being in an unfamiliar place and being alone can push Veterans into isolation and loneliness. Especially since as I mentioned earlier, we're such communal people. That's why there's a certain peace to having more solitude but when you're surrounded by people who don't speak your language, don't know you, it's easy to fall into the trap of expat isolation.

I moved abroad with already existing PTSD. Although going overseas was a big net positive when it came to my mental health, there were still challenges. Moving abroad can create a lot of internal turmoil, second guessing yourself and can worsen PTSD symptoms. Leaving America yanks you out of your current support system and can put you in a new area without your old friends or family. That's why it's important to build community abroad and to even get started on that mission before boarding a plane.

The combination of being in an unfamiliar place and having problems can be a tough adjustment for veterans. Getting yourself in and maintaining a routine can be a valuable tool to protect your mental health. I've found living overseas to be healthier and more peaceful, but I've witnessed veterans engage in personally destructive behaviors abroad as well.

12 Tips for Veteran Mental Health Abroad

- Get Connected: Join an expat social network, or club.
- Volunteer: Search for volunteer opportunities in your new location.
- Connect with nature and green spaces.
- Exercise.
- Manage your expectations. Life isn't perfect anywhere.

- Keep in contact with loved ones back home through technology.
- Discipline yourself with alcohol and unhealthy behaviors.
- Get over your FOMO of events in the states.
- Embrace new experiences, fill your time productively.
- Remember it's okay to be homesick.
- Enjoy the little things.
- Give yourself time to adjust.

Being overseas isn't an escape from your problems, but it can give you a new perspective on them. There's going to be stress with visas, language barriers, cultural problems and loneliness. There's a lot of stress with relocation and all it entails; it can be an overwhelming process. You are literally rebuilding your life in a new place

Sometimes it's good to go back to America for a little bit, I always end up going back once or twice a year and after a week or so I'm ready to head out. You can even get tired of going to the beach after a while and I see a lot of expats drinking or partying too much. It's easy to overindulge, eat too much, not engage in self-care and get homesick.

The first few months abroad can be the most difficult, be patient with your adjustment. Don't panic and don't think you have to do everything right away and have it all figured out. You also don't need to say yes to everything and it's important to have time to recharge to yourself. Having good friends to me is very important for my mental health, staying connected to the right kind of people.

I also do the things I like to do; I read books, write, swim and enjoy my own company. I live with a fellow veteran and that helps me have someone to talk to, someone to look out for me and someone to keep me accountable. I make my mental and spiritual health a priority because it's easy to get burned out living abroad.

When You're Struggling

- Be gentle with yourself
- Embrace your emotions, don't hide from them
- Enjoy your back home comforts abroad
- When you feel lost, get into nature
- Place importance on your sleep

Mental Health Resources

I've always believed in the power of affirmations for Veterans. We have a tendency to lean towards dark humor, sarcasm and embracing the suck. I have a

YouTube channel of Veteran Affirmations[58] including affirmations for PTSD, sleep meditations, and more for Veterans. Check out my book 365 Days of Veteran Affirmations[59] by yours truly.

The Veterans Crisis Line through the VA is always available, and you can chat, text, or call them. Check out Military OneSource's services that are confidential, short-term and 100% free. What I love about them is the different categories of support including relationships, family, money, and major changes. There are many other digital resources available for veteran mental health, you can reach out to people you served with, talk to your therapist, and more. Being abroad doesn't mean resources don't exist, you can access them through technology. Check out these mental health apps.

VA Mental Health Apps for Veterans[60]

Recognizing Culture Shock

- Anxiety
- Loneliness or feeling like an outcast
- Bad sleep patterns or routines

---

[58] https://www.youtube.com/@VeteranAffirmations

[59] https://a.co/d/gr8vvxg

[60] https://mobile.va.gov/appstore?filter%5Bapp_audience%5D=25

- Lack of motivation and feeling inadquate
- Big personality changes
- Lack of appetite

When you get abroad, even before you should be thinking of establishing your own support system. My friends and I do weekly dinners and that's one of the highlights of my week in the Dominican Republic, just a few good people getting a meal together and talking. In the United States it feels like nobody has time for conversation anymore but that's how you connect with people.

I've found abroad that I often have better conversations because people aren't always rushing around or doing a never-ending to do list or staring at their phones. It's easier to be more in the present moment and have time to enjoy the little things. Having a little culture shock is natural and as you get more comfortable certain things will fade. Make your mental health and self-care a priority for yourself in your new home. You aren't in the military anymore.

Chapter 30

Your New Home

If you feel panicked right away, that's normal. Be kind to yourself and just take your new life abroad one day at a time. A lot of homesickness might hit you that first week like a truck. Everything new around you will make you crave something familiar. When I get to Thailand for the first time, everything felt so foreign and exotic. I saw a McDonald's and went in and got a Big Mac and fries just to feel that American connection to something familiar.

That first week and first month make yourself a priority. You've created a new life for yourself and you're in a brand-new country. You're officially an expat and can add it to your resume of life experiences. Your past doesn't control you anymore and you're living in the moment.

Moving overseas doesn't make you a new person. But it's one of the biggest changes you can make to shift your life in a new direction. You're still you but your life will never be the same again. Whoever you say you are, you sort of are in your new location. A lot of who we are is impacted by where we are.

People don't know you or know anyone you know so the you that you put forward is the only one that exists. You can be someone with more patience, kindness, discipline or whatever you want to be. You can be more introverted or extroverted, Whatever version of you that you want to be you can be, how cool is that? You can't instantly change who you are but if you want to be someone who's more into fitness, golfer, baker or whatever else there's nothing holding you back from being that. You can paint or be a hippie or someone who reads more books.

It might seem like weird advice but first start in your new environment as a tourist. Go take some walking tours, look up the top things to do there and do all of them. Search Airbnb experiences and formal tours in your new area and learn everything from the ground up. These people can be a wealth of knowledge and great people to start off knowing.

The professional tour guides usually love where they live, that's what led them into their profession and often speak multiple languages. Visit museums and explore the history of your new location. Learn about the local life and visit small businesses in the area, introduce yourself to strangers and ask them about life.

Questions to ask locals

- What's your favorite thing about living here?

- What's something tourists don't know about in the area?
- What do you think is the best restaurant/coffee shop/grocery store?
- What do you wish people knew about this place?
- Where's the best place for me to live around here?

You won't learn the ins and outs of the place without asking questions. Do some people watching your first few months and learn about their holidays and customs. One small reason I love living abroad is because I can celebrate all the holidays in the Dominican Republic and the holidays I grew up with in the United States. I remember feeling stupid asking my Dominican friend what he was going to do for Thanksgiving, like duh John Dominicans don't do Thanksgiving.

Culture Shock

Everything feels brand new and foreign because it is brand new and foreign. You're in a new country and some small things will stand out to you. Some of these things might even bother you or make you uncomfortable. Focus on the positive, not what's negative or what's missing in your new environment. A lot of people get worked up when they can't find something like the kind of deodorant or cereal they like. Get to know a variety of different types of people and try to be outgoing. Be open and accepting things that even seem backwards.

New Location Tips

- Find out the closest emergency room.
- Get together with other expats, start by meeting people from Facebook groups.
- Balance yourself and find your healthy equilibrium in your new home.
- Expect to feel homesick now and then
- Make sure you know where the closest emergency room is.

Nothing Is Forever

There might come a time when you need to go home. You might have an unexpected life event, illness, or other unforeseen circumstances. Moving back home after living abroad can be tough, you go through a reverse culture shock. A lot of expats never want to think about going back to America because they love their lives abroad, but sometimes things go wrong.

Some adventures come to an end, a lot of people choose to live abroad for a few years and then feel the pull to return to America. Sometimes the longer you're overseas, the harder it becomes to move home. It's not a failure going home, moving back can be part of life's journey.

You'll always view America differently after living abroad.

Your New Routine

Other expats are busy too, just as busy as they were in America but it's a different kind of schedule. Your daily itinerary is fuller of social activities, you have scuba dive trips, tee times, dinner parties, concerts, and festivals. It's going to include more things you want to do instead of what you need to do.

1. Wake up at the same time.
2. Set a schedule.
3. Develop a fitness routine.
4. Set small goals.
5. Make your new life fun.

You made it, congrats. You're living a new and exciting life. You're a veteran expat and you've done something most people would never dream of doing.

The Final Word

Conclusion

I wanted this book to be your jumping off point, to open your eyes to the idea of living abroad. The goal was to give you a lot of practical advice, information and knowledge about moving and living abroad as a Veteran. Before taking the jump yourself, there's more country specific homework you'll need to do, and everyone's situation is going to be different. What's worked for me isn't going to work for everyone.

I'm frustrated with the rising individualism of America, the political class, and military leadership. I'm mad about the lack of accountability for so called important people and Generals and the over-accountability for the little people and Privates. I'm not pleased with the direction the military has taken in recent years regarding some things, but the military will always mirror society.

I do know that during my service and yours we were sent on a roller coaster of incoherent policies in our conflicts. We, as defenders of the republic, deserved better than what we received from our politicians and leaders. We didn't fight wars for twenty plus years to live in a country at war with itself.

I stumbled into veterans abroad stuff and I truly appreciate the positive response, emails, and messages I've received from veterans. I even appreciate the negativity because it lets me know I'm onto something.

I realized there was a big gap of information regarding supply and demand of veterans living abroad content and information. I appreciate all the help I can get to provide resources and information to our brother and sister veterans. If you've got resources, I should share on social media or include in my work please reach out.

If you're a veteran living abroad, connect with me on social media so we can support one another. I love America, her ideals and the constitution. Like most veterans I'm honored to have worn the uniform and fought for my country and its values.

I really miss a lot of things about the Army, especially some of the people I served with. Writing can feel like a lonely process. Even though I write to connect with other Veterans, it's something that demands a certain level of solitude and introspection. I worked hard on this.

I'm going to ask you to check me out on social media, follow my platforms and scope out my creative projects. Subscribe to my free living abroad newsletter to continue to get updated information about life abroad for US Veterans. We live in a social media world, so I'd appreciate you sharing this guide with a fellow Veteran, a video from my Instagram or TikTok or an article from my blog. I will continue to work hard for the Veteran community and I appreciate your support.

I appreciate the Veterans that collaborated with me to create this and the incredible community of Veterans living here in the beautiful Dominican Republic. I'd also like to thank my mother for her unwavering support of my endeavors, both in uniform and as a civilian. Thank you to my battle buddy Keith Pyron aka SGT Sosua for being the original founder of Veterans in Paradise and working hard for our brothers and sisters in arms.

Thanks again to you for reading my work,

Thank you once again for your service,

John

Veterans Abroad Resources

Websites

www.poppinsmoke.com – I've referenced this a few times throughout this book. Created by Army spouse Stephanie, it has a ton of information on using your military benefits to travel. You'll especially want to check this out if you want to explore Space A Travel.

https://www.crewdogs.com/- This is essentially Airbnb but only for the military community. Created by Vets for Vets. It's a great resource for cheap stays and each stay gives back to a Veteran charity.

VeteransinParadise.com – This is a website ran by myself and my friend SFC Retired Keith Pyron. Sign up for our free newsletter to learn more about Veterans moving and living abroad.

https://libo-risk.com/ - Liborisk is a great travel community for the Veteran community. They host events, retreats and more both in the states and abroad. Creating by a Marine Veteran, it's worth checking out if you want to travel and connect with fellow Veterans.

https://www.afvclub.com/ - Armed Forces Vacation Club is a free membership travel club for active and retired military plus Veterans. They have a lot of great deals for the Veteran community.

https://www.americanforcestravel.com/ - American Forces Travel, supported by Priceline, is the U.S. Department of Defense official online leisure travel site for active military, Guard or Reserve, U.S. Coast Guard, Retired military, and all eligible MWR patrons.

American Legions Abroad

https://www.legion.org/about/organization/fodpal - The website for Fodpal (Foreign and Outlying Departments and posts of the American Legion)

Individual Post Links

Chapala Mexico American Legion Post 7[61]

Puerto Vallarta Mexico Instagram Post 12[62]

Merida Yucatan Mexico American Legion Post[63]

American Legion Costa Rica[64]

American Legion in Puerto Rico[65]

American Legion Stuttgart Germany[66]

---

[61] https://www.facebook.com/LegionLakeChapalaPost7/

[62] https://www.instagram.com/legionpost12mx/

[63] https://www.facebook.com/groups/831539920846143/

[64] https://www.facebook.com/amlegioncr/

[65] https://www.facebook.com/legionprorg/

[66] https://www.facebook.com/Post6Stuttgart/

American Legion Ansbach Germany[67]

American Legion Department of France

American Legion Okinawa Japan[68]

American Legion South Korea[69]

American Legion Thailand TH01 Udon Ratchathini[70]

American Legion Thailand TH02 Pattaya[71]

American Legion Thailand Bangkok

---

[67] https://www.facebook.com/AmericanLegionPost1982/

[68] https://www.facebook.com/okipost28/

[69] https://www.facebook.com/LLMPost38/

[70] https://www.facebook.com/americanlegionthailandpostth01/

[71] https://www.facebook.com/groups/189305839175725/

Department of Philippines American Legion[72]

American Legion Auxiliary Philippines[73]

Note: There are other American Legion posts abroad. These are ones with an active site or social media presence.

Veterans of Foreign Wars Posts Abroad

https://oms.vfw.org/findapost/foreign.aspx   -   This website will direct you to a foreign post directory.

VFW Department of Europe[74]

Individual Post Links

VFW Cambodia[75]

---

[72]   https://www.facebook.com/p/Department-of-Philippines-American-Legion-100068195300715/

[73] https://www.facebook.com/alaphilippines/

[74]   https://www.facebook.com/p/VFW-Department-of-Europe-100064638794590/

[75] https://vfw11575.org/di/vfw/v2/default.asp

VFW France[76]

VFW Germany Weisbaden[77]

VFW Germany Illesheim[78]

VFW Germany Grafenwoehr[79]

VFW Germany Erlangen[80]

VFW Germany Donnersburg[81]

---

[76] https://vfw605.org/di/vfw/v2/default.asp

[77] https://www.facebook.com/watchontherhein/

[78] https://www.facebook.com/groups/344527705565541/

[79] https://www.facebook.com/TowerPost10692/

[80] https://www.facebook.com/VFWPost3885/

[81] https://www.facebook.com/VFWPost3885/

VFW Italy The Mediterranean Post[82]

VFW Japan Yokosuka

VFW Korea[83]

VFW Philippines Angeles[84]

VFW Philippines Manila[85]

VFW Philippines Bauang Sur[86]

VFW Philippines Baguio City[87]

---

[82] https://www.facebook.com/VFW.MediterraneanPost8862/

[83] https://www.facebook.com/vfw10223/

[84] https://www.facebook.com/VFW2485/

[85] https://www.facebook.com/groups/vfwmanila/?locale=es_ES

[86] https://www.facebook.com/vfw9892/

[87] https://www.facebook.com/groups/VFW124/

VFW Philippines Palawan[88]

VFW Philippines Cebu[89]

VFW Puerto Rico Anasco[90]

VFW Taiwan[91]

VFW Thailand Pattaya[92]

VFW Thailand Chiang Mai[93]

VFW Australia[94]

---

[88] https://www.facebook.com/groups/1035125564206850/

[89] https://www.facebook.com/groups/728340752280820/

[90] https://www.facebook.com/p/VFW-Post-11103-A%C3%B1asco-PR-100086771469293/

[91]
https://www.facebook.com/www.vfwflyingtigerpost9957taipeitaiwan.org/

[92] https://www.facebook.com/post9876/?locale=th_TH

[93] https://www.facebook.com/groups/chiangmaivfw/

[94] https://www.facebook.com/vfw12163/

Note: There are more Veterans of Foreign Wars Posts overseas. These are the ones with an active site or social media presence.

YouTube Channels

Combat Vet Abroad – My own YouTube.

SGT Sosua – Creator of Veterans in Paradise SFC Retired Keith Pyron.

Honestly, I don't really know many YouTube channels about Veterans moving and living abroad. If you do have some Veteran channels, let me know so I can add resources in the future. One of the reasons I finally made a YouTube channel was because I realized a lot of people just aren't going to read a long book like this.

Facebook Groups

US Military Retirees and Veterans Living Overseas[95]

Veterans of Puerto Vallarta Mexico[96]

---

[95] https://www.facebook.com/groups/MilitaryVeteransOverseas/

[96] https://www.facebook.com/groups/1284766768547942/

Veterans in Paradise (Dominican Republic)[97]

US Vets Living in Thailand and FMP[98]

US Service Connected Veterans in the Philippines[99]

Veteran Expats Living in Mexico

Veteran Expats of Colombia[100]

FMP For Veterans Traveling Abroad[101]

US Veterans in the Philippines[102]

---

[97] https://www.facebook.com/groups/1144729350028386

[98] https://www.facebook.com/groups/USVetsInThailand

[99] https://www.facebook.com/groups/548664582567218

[100] https://www.facebook.com/groups/2223891227629431

[101] https://www.facebook.com/groups/fmpworldwide

[102] https://www.facebook.com/groups/6206012226091081/

Expat US Veterans in Costa Rica[103]

US Military Veterans Living and Retiring in Thailand[104]

US Veterans in Medellin, Colombia[105]

That's all folks, enjoy your life – You deserve it.

John

---

[103] https://www.facebook.com/groups/1555134184681458

[104] https://www.facebook.com/groups/298419135499094

[105] https://www.facebook.com/groups/343667793346859

www.ingramcontent.com/pod-product-compliance
Lightning Source LLC
Chambersburg PA
CBHW061817040426
42447CB00012B/2699